The Making of the Couple

The Making of the Couple

The Social Function of Short-Form Medieval Narrative

A Symposium

Odense University Press 1991

The publication of this volume was made possible by the generous support of the Danish Research Council for the Humanities

Proceedings of the Fifteenth International Symposium organized by the Centre for the Study of Vernacular Literature in the Middle Ages held at Odense University on 19–20 November, 1990

Edited by
Flemming G. Andersen
Morten Nøjgaard

The Cover:
Psalterium Feriatum
Gent-Brügge 1500-1535
The Royal Library
Copenhagen

© *Odense University Press 1991*
Printed by AiO Tryk, Odense
Cover by Ulla Poulsen Precht
ISBN 87 7492 847 3

Contents

Preface and Acknowledgements

The papers presented in this volume were given at the symposium *The Making of the Couple. The Social Function of Short-Form Medieval Narrative* organized by Odense University's Centre for the Study of Vernacular Literature in the Middle Ages, 19 - 20 November, 1990. We are grateful to the authors and to all the other members of the symposium for their contribution to the success of the symposium; to the Carlsberg Foundation and to The Danish Research Council for the Humanities for the financial support which made the symposium possible.

We should also like to thank Connie Beck, without whom neither symposium nor book would have come to successful fruition, and Anette Thingholm, who helped Connie Beck in the practical task of running the symposium. Furthermore, as always but with increasing gratitude, we wish to thank the staff of Odense University Press for advice and assistance in the preparation of this volume.

The Editors

La formation du couple: La témoignage du conte médiéval.

Le moyen âge jette les bases de la société moderne – aussi dans le domaine de la vie privée, créant les règles de la convivialité et du commerce amoureux, règles qui continuent à scander le rythme de nos jours. Importantes entre toutes, les normes qui président à la formation du couple érotique formé par un homme et une femme suivent un parcours historique mal élucidé. On connaît le résultat qui émane au grand jour vers la fin du XVIIIe siècle: le mariage d'amour basé sur le libre choix des partenaires et sur une communauté mystique de corps et d'âme, mais on ignore l'origine de cet étrange phénomène composite. On suit certes relativement bien l'évolution de certains éléments, mais comment scruter les reins et les coeurs des jeunes gens du haut moyen âge florissant, époque décisive de l'émergence d'une nouvelle conception globale du phénomène amoureux? Soutenus par les théologiens, les juristes et, surtout, les poètes, ce sont ces gens qui, peu à peu, ont porté un état finalement fort prosaïque, le mariage, à un degré d'idéalité mystique étonnant, transformant par là radicalement l'idée que l'on pouvait se faire du couple érotique.

On ignorera toujours les états d'esprit des damoiseaux et des damoiselles, mais il n'en reste pas moins légitime de regarder la littérature narrative médiévale comme un miroir ou plutôt un reflet – plus ou moins fidèle – de ces états d'âme, comme un champ d'essai où les poètes soumettaient les normes naissantes à l'épreuve de la narrativité, c.-à-d. de l'expérience vitale. Voilà l'objectif que s'est proposé le symposium "The Making of the Couple, the Social Function of Short-Form Medieval Narrative". La thème a été illustré par des conférenciers venus d'horizons divers, mais tous animés par le désir d'examiner dans quelle mesure une certaine idée du couple amoureux était en gestation dans la littérature médiévale de leur spécialité.

En effet, il est indéniable qu'à partir tout au moins du XIIIe siècle, les formes narratives courtes tournent avec une véritable obsession autour des multiples problèmes soulevés par les rapports amoureux, notamment dans leurs relations, toujours hautement problématiques, avec l'institution du mariage. A partir des fabliaux français, le symposium a suivi les vicissitudes de ces rapports à travers les contes allemands, italiens et anglais, tout en esquissant les limites d'une telle investigation: la littérature nordique semble bien envisager les problèmes du couple dans une autre optique que celle du mariage d'amour, et les livres de famille florentins du moyen âge finissant attestent le clivage qui a dû exister entre les conceptualisations des conteurs et la réalité de la vie vécue.

Ce dernier fait suffirait à lui tout seul à nous mettre en garde contre les embûches dont est semé le chemin d'une investigation de ce type. Si le conte est un reflet des mutations spirituelles profondes qui s'opèrent au cours du moyen âge dans le domaine de la vie privée, rien ne nous garantit que les intrigues divertissantes ou morales des conteurs représentent autre chose que des fantaisies plus ou moins gratuites.

Le fait spirituel fondamental demeure. A un moment donné on a imaginé de mettre en rapport la sexualité, qui ne pouvait donner naissance qu'à des couples éphémères, avec le couple marié, institution créée pour assurer la perpétuation de l'espèce et de la famille et qui avait donc la vocation de durer le temps d'une vie. Quand cette fusion s'est-elle opérée et sous quelles formes et à quel rythme a-t-elle pris racine dans les mentalités? Seule la littérature pourra nous offrir des éléments de réponse à ces questions – à condition de procéder avec la prudence nécessaire commandée par le statut esthétique et social spécifique des textes narratifs courts.

D'abord on observe que ces textes n'observent pas nécessairement l'idéologie réellement en vigueur à l'époque de leur création. Il faut faire la part de l'originalité créatrice de chaque conteur et de son degré variable de conformisme. Ensuite, il va sans dire que la symbolisation littéraire suit ses lois esthétique propres, brodant sur des canevas souvent fort traditionnels et qui ne traduisent donc en rien une quelconque réalité. En outre, une très grande partie des contes traitant du couple appartient à des registres comiques ou satiriques. Or, on sait bien que le comique trouve sa source beaucoup moins dans des phénomènes réels que dans des situations archétypales, pour ainsi dire, et dont la valeur de témoignage est mince. Enfin, la société médiévale, en constante mutation, reste une société d'ordres, et les règles qui président au choix du partenaire matrimonial diffèrent du tout au tout selon le statut social. Ainsi il est évident que les paysans et les bourgeois qui évoluent dans les contes n'engagent que très modérément les membres de la chevalerie: ceux-ci se sont sans doute bien divertis de ces comportements bizarres qui juraient avec les leurs.

Ainsi les études qu'on va lire ne décrivent ni les réalités sociales des couples moyenâgeux, ni les suprastructures idéologiques dont les ordres entouraient et justifiaient l'organisation sociale de leur état, mais simplement les symbolisations narratives que les conteurs médiévaux nous proposent de la formation du couple et de l'évolution des rapports amoureux. Ces recherches demandent à être complétées par un examen non seulement des autres genres narratifs, mais aussi des textes juridiques, théologiques historiques. Ainsi seulement pourra-ton espérer aboutir à une image nuancée et fidèle de la sociogenèse de cette cellule sociale sur laquelle repose notre modernité: le couple amoureux fondateur de famille, cellule qui, en cette fin de siècle, est peut-être en train de perdre son statut fondamental et qui, en tout cas, est en but, de nouveau, à de profondes mutations.

Le comité de rédaction

Les problemes du couple
Une Réalité voilée

Par MICHEL OLSEN, *Université de Roskilde*

Introduction

Cet essai, légère adaptation de ma conférence, suivra un chemin quelque peu tortueux. Après une présentation de quelques problèmes généraux – demandée en guise d'introduction au congrès – j'esquisserai brièvement ma conception de l'argumentation narrative dans le genre de la nouvelle, après quoi, posant la question de la réalité, du vécu quotidien, j'irai à sa recherche chez un nouvelliste 'populaire', Giovanni Sercambi.

Amour, mariage et christianisme

Pour comprendre les problèmes du couple au cours du Moyen Age, il faut probablement tenir présente l'aversion de l'Église pour l'amour courtois, et l'aversion du code courtois pour le mariage. Je demande la permission d'un rappel d'une problématique bien connu – et que j'illustrerai par le moyen d'un seul exemple – mais qui, à être oublié, fausserait gravement nos discussions.

Dans le premier christianisme, certains avaient combattu les tendances ascétiques. Un certain Jovinien avait avancé que l'amour dans le mariage valait bien l'état virginal. Il eut droit à la réfutation du *Contre Jovinien* de saint Jérôme. Depuis, l'amour physique, même réalisé dans le mariage, n'a été accepté par l'Église qu'à des conditions limitatives: procréation, modération, etc. L'état virginal préconisé par le christianisme conflue avec la louange de l'état d'indépendance vanté par les philosophes de l'Antiquité païenne. Dans les deux cas, le célibat (avec ou sans voeu de chasteté) est préférable, et de beaucoup, au mariage. C'est ce qui ressort des lettres d'Héloïse à Abailard: le mariage ne convient pas à la dignité d'un clerc.[1] *L'Anti-Jovinien*, dont Héloïse reprend

---

[1] Philippe Delhaye: "Le Dossier anti-matrimonial de l'"Adversum Jovinianum" et son influence sur quelques écrits du IIe siècle".. *Mediaeval Studies* 13, 1951, pp. 65-86 1951.

Saint Jérôme veut montrer 1º que le Nouveau Testament préconise l'état virginal, 2º que telle est aussi la préférence de L'Ancien Testament, 3º que la tradition païenne a tenu la

l'argumentation, avance ainsi certains arguments contre le mariage en vogue depuis l'antiquité. Héloïse va jusqu'à préférer le statut d''amica' (maîtresse), voire de 'meretrix' (maîtresse passagère) à celui de femme mariée, et cela pour préserver la dignité de son bien-aimé![2]

On ne trouve pas, à ma connaissance, dans la culture de l'Église, une valorisation de l'amour ni de l'amour dans le mariage. Et le libéralisme de certains hérétiques semblent encore plus opposé à l'amour physique. Seulement, comme la chair est le mal, le mariage ne saurait sanctifier ou rendre admissible ce qui est condamné d'avance.

Dans la doctrine officielle, les justifications de l'amour dans mariage semblent s'en tenir à l'importance de la procréation, ainsi qu'à l'entraide que se doivent mari et femme. Et il est rare de trouver les problèmes du couple au centre de l'argumentation.

La Courtoisie

Il est tentant d'aller chercher des renseignements sur le couple dans la littérature courtoise et dans la nouvelle, qui reprend et modifie les valeurs de la courtoisie. Les deux courants focalisent l'intérêt sur les problèmes du couple. La littérature courtoise se concentre sur les rapports entre les amoureux et la nouvelle y ajoute, le plus souvent sur le registre comique, ceux entre mari et femme.

Comme je le rappellerai brièvement, le traitement que reçoivent les problèmes du couple dans ces littératures, sont de l'ordre de l'utopie, ce qui n'exclut nullement une mise en question explicite ou implicite de la réalité sociale. Il est impossible, comme on le sait, de saisir directement la réalité sociale dans la littérature. Qui plus est, il se pourrait que littérature courtoise et nouvelle aristocratique nous renseignent moins que certains autres genres sur ce que furent les relations du couple.

Pour notre propos, l'on peut définir l'amour courtois de façon assez large: dans l'amour courtois, les rapports entre les amoureux deviennent un des enjeux

---

virginité en haute estime, 4º que les philosophes Aristote, Sénèque, Plutarque aurait eu la même préférence (en fait, comme le dit Delahaye, saint Jérôme cite surtout le néoplatonicien Porphyre). Une question se pose: tout en admettant le mariage, Jovinien a-t-il reconnu une quelque valeur humaine à l'amour? Il semble que non. Cf. aussi Michel Foucault: *Histoire de la sexualité I: La Volonté de savoir, II: L'Usage des plaisirs*, III: *Le Souci de soi*. Gallimard, Paris 1976, 1980, 1984.

2   Pierre Abélard & Héloïse: *Mine trængslers historie.* efterfulgt af As og Hs breve. indledninger af Olaf Pedersen. Falkeserien. Reitzel, Copenhague 1954 p. 84.

les plus importants de la vie. Je crois que cette idée simple pourra suffire pour ce qui suivra. L'autre enjeu est, comme déjà avant la courtoisie, l'honneur. Les deux valeurs sont d'ailleurs intimement liées.

L'amour courtois ne change tout d'abord rien au jugement porté sur le mariage, si ce n'est dans le sens d'une négligence encore plus prononcée. Il est, depuis son commencement, anti-matrimonial: la poésie des troubadours et les premiers romans de Tristan l'indiquent clairement. Dans la courtoisie même, le mythe (ou le roman) de Tristan va pourtant bientôt poser des problèmes, et l'amour asocial à la manière de Tristan et d'Yseult est combattu par un Chrétien de Troyes et d'autres. L'amour courtois devient possible dans le mariage, mais dès l'apparition du mariage d'amour, celui-ci est chargé d'une fonction sociale. Dans les premiers romans courtois, les mariages relient riches et pauvres, toujours à l'intérieur de la noblesse.[3] Puis on en arrive, dans la littérature courtoise tardive, à des solutions de conflits qui, considérées sous le rapport des valeurs narrativement affirmées, sont on ne peut plus conformistes: les amoureux épousent des partenaires de rang égal: ceux que le système social leur prescrit (état des choses qui se prolonge, avec de rares exceptions, jusqu'à nos jours, ou presque). Parallèlement se développent les invectives contre les roturiers qui obtiennent des honneurs sociales (et, curieusement, la figure de la femme malfaisante se développe corrélativement).

Dans la courtoisie tardive, l'on se trouve ainsi dans une situation curieuse: l'amour est possible dans le mariage, mais, semble-t-il, seulement dans les couches sociales nobles. Je me suis risqué à faire une large synthèse – qui n'est peut-être qu'une vue de l'esprit – mais à titre d'indice on pourrait citer *Les Miracles de Nostre Dame par personnages*.[4] Dans ces 40 pièces de théâtre datant du XIVe siècle, on trouve une dramatisation d'un certain nombre de romans courtois tardifs (ou de légendes) dont la trame est tissée par la séparation et les retrouvailles d'un mari et d'une femme qui sont roi et reine. Il y est incontestablement question d'amour entre mari et femme. Or ces pièces étaient destinées à un public bourgeois, la guilde des orfèvres de Paris. Ces bourgeois ont-ils célébré l'amour matrimonial par procuration?[5]

---

3   Erich Köhler: *Ideal und Wirklichkeit in der höfischen Epik*. M. Niemeyer Verlag, Tübingen 1970.

4   Gustave Lanson: & Ulysse Robert (éd): *Miracles de Nostre Dame par personnages, d'après le manuscrit de la bibliothèque nationale*. Société des Anciens Textes Français, Paris 1876-1883.

5   Cf.Michel Olsen: "Miracles de Nostre Dame par personnages". *Popular Drama in the Northern Europe in the Later Middle Ages. A Symposium* éd. Flemming G. Andersen et al. Odense University Press, 1988, pp.41-63.

L'Argumentation narrative
La Nouvelle de Boccace

La nouvelle créée par Boccace se rapporte de façon incontestable à la courtoisie, même si elle s'oppose à certains aspects de cette culture courtoise. En ce qui concerne les nouvelles traitant du mariage, non seulement l'amour y est souvent représenté en termes courtois; il y constitue aussi un enjeu d'importance vitale, et les deux partenaires sont individualisés et invitent à l'identification. L'amour courtois conventionnel, souvent réalisé physiquement, se prolonge ainsi, à travers le XVIIIe, presque jusqu'à nos jours.[6] Le groupe de nouvelles auquel je pense traite de deux jeunes gens non-mariés qui s'aiment et qui veulent se marier, voire réaliser des rapports extra-matrimoniaux. Qu'ils réussissent ou non, leurs amours sont toujours pris au sérieux et ils sont investis de la sympathie, du moins relative, de l'auteur. Même dans les nouvelles où l'amant a recours à la ruse, l'objet courtisé est toujours relativement respecté: la dame reste ou redevient dame presque dans le sens de la poésie courtoise.

Quand il s'agit du mari, les choses changent. Dans la grande majorité des cas, le mari est cocufié et tend par là à devenir ridicule. Il y a probablement plusieurs raisons à cela: le mariage comme lieu de la réalisation érotique est une invention moderne. En plus, il y a une raison triviale et structurale: les époux vivent ensemble; normalement ils ne sauraient donc devenir des objets narratifs: des objets d'une quête, l'un pour l'autre. Les cas d'exception confirment cette observation: on trouve l'amour posé entre mari et femme du moment qu'ils sont séparés par des événements malheureux.[7] Pourtant la maîtrise de Boccace va jusqu'à savoir combiner la réalisation de l'adultère avec le souci de la vie menacée d'une mari. Tedaldo degli Elisei réussit à récupérer l'amour de sa bien-aimée tout en sauvant la vie du mari de celle-ci.[8]

Dans le *Décaméron*, Boccace est permissif: on y trouve dans une mesure extraordinaire, soit dans le mariage, soit dans les relations extramatrimoniales, la réunion entre les classes et groupes sociaux différents. Une telle constatation résulte d'une comparaison avec la tradition de la nouvelle postérieure à Boccace.[9]

---

[6] Un Racine, chez qui le désir a souvent recours au pouvoir, voire à la violence morale, les termes de la courtoisie sont toujours en vigueur.

[7] Nouvelles II,6; X,9. Je cite d'après: Giovanni Boccaccio: *Il Decameron. Tutte le opere di G.B.* vol. 4, éd. Vittore Branca. I Classici Mondadori. 1976.

[8] III,7.

[9] Cette constatation est d'ailleurs d'interprétation difficile. Il n'y a rien chez Boccace d'un révolutionnaire (d'ailleurs les écrivains révolutionnaires ne s'occupent pas d'établir d'abord

La Nouvelle post-boccacienne

Dans la combinaisons des partenaires, soit dans le mariage, soit dans des relations libres ou adultérines, Boccace avait été un libéral. Il combine les représentants des différentes classes, tantôt en faisant réussir leurs amours, tantôt en les faisant échouer, mais tragiquement (et le tragique garde la sympathie aux malheureux amants).

Or les épigones, contrairement à une vue qui a encore cours (mais que les études précises réfutent de plus en plus[10]), ne reprennent que rarement les structures complexes.

La tradition de la nouvelle, créée par le chef-d'oeuvre de Boccace, reprend, avec quelques notables exceptions, la matière dont fourmille le *Décaméron*. On peut, comme je l'ai tenté, essayer de donner une typologie des intrigues les plus fréquentes:[11]

1º on fait la cour, 2º on cherche à obtenir l'amour par ruse (ou violence), 3º Les amoureux sont d'accord. ils s'adonnent à l'adultère, ou bien des jeunes gens cherchent à s'unir dans le mariage.

Toutefois, depuis Boccace, dans un nombre important de recueils, les valeurs

---

et avant tout l'égalité dans l'amour); tout au plus pourrait-on avancer qu'il cherche, en combinant dans son utopie ces différents groupes, à sauvegarder l'unité d'une société communale menacée (mais cette interprétation – qui est aussi la mienne (cf. *Les transformations du Triangle érotique*. Akademisk forlag, Copenhague 1976 et *Amore Virtú e Potere nella novellistica rinascimentale. Argomentazione narrativa e ricezione letteraria.* Federico & Ardia, Napoli 1984). peut facilement être contestée. Se posent au moins deux questions: quelle fut l'attitude politique de Boccace? et, si l'on arrive à répondre à cette première question: peut-on établir une relation de cause à effet entre les convictions politiques d'un auteur et son chef-d'oeuvre. Je passe sur une troisième question: les convictions politiques de Boccace n'ont-elles pas varié durant sa longue vie, question qui touche à la deuxième, car une oeuvre n'est peut-être pas contemporaine aux attitudes politiques de leur auteur. On n'a qu'à considérer les nombreux auteurs qui furent communistes: leurs oeuvres n'expriment pas toujours, loin de là! la vulgate marxiste.

10 Ainsi, pour Sercambi, qui va nous occuper tout à l'heure, L. Rossi et G. Sinicropi ont bien montré que cet auteur ne se contente nullement de copier. Cf. G. Sinicropi: "La questione degli epigoni" in *Boccaccio: secoli di vita*, éd. Cottino Jones, Ravenna 1977 et L. Rossi: "Sercambi e Boccaccio". *Studi sul Boccaccio VI* 1971 pp. 145-179 ainsi que l'introduction à son édition des nouvelles de Sercambi (v. ci-dessous). J'ai développé moi-même cette idée dans "Copista o creatore? Giovanni Sercambi riscrive l'ultima novella del *Decameron*". *Analecta romana instituti danici XVII-XVIII*, p. 127-132 1989a. (Chose curieuse: dans toutes ces comparaisons, il y a très peu de redites. Il faut bien croire que l'on compare par rapport, souvent implicite, à une idée pré-conçue).

11 *Les Transformations ... et Amore...*

ont fondamentalement changé. De façon très simplificatrice , on peut résumer la tendance générale ainsi: en ce qui concerne le mariage et les relations non-adultérines, l'amour sérieux, ou tragique (dans les deux cas la sympathie suit les amoureux), se développe entre partenaires qui, socialement, sont approximativement égaux (les familles de Romeo et Juliette sont de la même noblesse).[12] L'amant inférieur, cherchant à pénétrer dans les hautes couches sociales, est le plus souvent sévèrement puni, mais il n'y a guère que le *Novellino* de Masuccio salernitano qui va jusqu'à admettre qu'un grand noble puisse user de violence envers un bourgeois, emportant sa femme et son argent.[13] Même dans les *Cent Nouvelles Nouvelles*, à première vue si libérales, les rares exemples qui traitent du mariage entre jeunes semblent assez conservatrices: l'égalité sociale y est de règle.

Malgré les réserves que l'on doit faire quant à l'identité structurale entre modèles et épigones, on peut esquisser un système d'argumentation narrative qui vaut pour écrire une grande partie des nouvelles depuis Boccace et jusqu'à la Contre-Réforme.

Il semble bien que l'argumentation narrative primitive du récit bref (type *exemplum* ou nouvelle embryonnaire) est l'argumentation par négation, l'exemplum deterrens[14] En ce qui concerne la fable antique, une action est proposée aux lecteurs et cette action est évaluée négativement.[15] Ainsi rien que par sa position, la première action décrite est structuralement désigné à être désapprouvée. Nous verrons une tendance vers cette structure simple chez un Sercambi. (Le récit bref à argumentation positive, qui ne nous occupera pas ici, semble prédominer dans les vies de saints, et on le trouve dans la nouvelle dès son origine (le *Novellino* en contient des occurrences).[16]

Le genre de la nouvelle développe l'argumentation narrative par un système

---

12 Pourtant, une certaine différence de rang, à l'intérieur de la noblesse, peut donner lieu à des nouvelles tragiques, ainsi chez Masuccio salernitano: cf. *Les Transformations* ... pp. 142 ss. & *Il Novellino*, éd. G. Petrocchi, Firenze 1957, reprint 1975, éd. Salvatore S. Nigro 1957, nouvelles 31, 33, 35.

13 Cf. *Transformations*... pp. 139 ss.

14 Cf. Piotr Salwa: "Retorica e politica – *Croniche e novelle* di Giovanni Sercambi, lucchese. *Renaissance Studies in Honor of Craig Hugh Smyth* 1985, p.469 qui cite C. Perelman: *L'Empire rhétorique. Rhétorique et argumentation*. Paris 1977 et A. Vitale-Brovarone: "Persuasione e narrazione. L'exemplum tra due retoriche". *Mélanges de l'École française de Rome*, xcii, pp. 87-112 1980.

15 Morten Nøjgaard: *La Fable antique* vol. I. Copenhague 1964.

16 Je passe sous silence les nombreux récits qui argumente aussi bien par négation que par affirmation, distribuant ces argumentations contraires sur deux ou plusieurs protagonistes.

d'affirmations et de négations qui s'enchaînent et se nuancent entre elles, mettant sur pied un système argumentatif assez compliqué.

Dès le *Décaméron* ce système est presque entièrement en place. Mais au cours de son évolution (ou involution comme on voudra) le genre de la nouvelle, en grande partie créé par Boccace, se distingue du chef- d'oeuvre de ce dernier à plusieurs égards.

En ce qui nous concerne ici, nous pouvons retenir deux points: La nouvelle, après la permissivité de Boccace, revient presque aussitôt, comme je viens de le dire, vers un rappel à l'ordre. En plus, elle développe de façon assez compliquée l'argumentation argumentative. Celle-ci reste toujours fondamentalement liée aux catégories succès *vs* échec, mais elle est progressivement compliquée, notamment par l'importance accrue accordée aux modifications de volonté, à la conversion aux valeurs morales.[17]

Pour une considération plus générale, bien des nouvelles post- boccacciennes usent ainsi d'une argumentation narrative aussi bien que les *exempla*. Mais cette argumentation se situe souvent à deux niveaux. A un premier niveau, les valeurs des protagonistes (beauté, plaisir, bien-être matériel) sont gagnants et la libération des désirs plus ou moins réalisée. A un deuxième niveau, les valeurs de la société sont implicitement ou explicitement affirmés: égalité des conditions dans le mariage, exclusion des couches inférieures.

Contrairement aux *exempla*, les nouvelles n'illustrent pas nécessairement une doctrine (mais rien n'empêche qu'elles assument cette fonction): De façon plus précise, on peut dire qu'elles ne figurent pas insérées dans un texte de type différent, didactique (traité, sermon), à moins de considérer les cadres des recueils comme un type de texte autre, ce qui me semble parfois tout à fait indiqué. On peut également caractériser la nouvelle par l'autonomie qu'elle gagne par rapport aux genres avoisinants.[18] Toujours reste-t-il que les relations entre *exemplum* et nouvelle sont loin d'être simples.

D'autre part, comme le fait Wetzel,[19] il est plausible d'avancer qu'à la Renais-

---

[17] Il semble que durant la Contre-Réforme il ne suffise pas que les bonnes valeurs (de l'ordre ans le mariage etc.) soient affirmées: il faut, en plus, réintégrer dans la bonne société les protagonistes des couches sociales supérieures qui ont commis (ou risqué commettre) une faute (alors que les protagonistes des basses couches sociales sont systématiquement punis.

[18] Cf. Hans Jürgen Neuschäfer: *Boccaccio und der Beginn der Novelle*. München 1969, et Cesare Segre: *"La novella e i generi letterari"*. *La Novella Italiana. Atti del convegno di Caprarola 19-24 settembre 1988* vol. I, Salerno editrice, Roma 1989.

[19] Hermann H. Wetzel: "Premesse per una storia del genere della novella. La novella romanza del Due al Seicento". *La Novella Italiana. Atti del convegno di Caprarola 19-24 settembre 1988* vol. I, Salerno editrice, Roma 1989.

sance le récit bref se retrouve englobé dans des types de textes non-narratifs, mais que ces textes sont radicalement différents des textes didactiques qui enchassent les *exempla* classiques (le cadre où l'on discute de *L'Heptaméron* de Marguerite de Navarre, les *Essais* de Montaigne enchassent des récits qui, contredisant souvent le texte englobant, sont autant de départs pour une discussion dont l'éventuel résultat n'est pas l'essentiel; le récit, *exemplum* ou nouvelle comme on voudra, devient un énigme plutôt que la preuve d'une doctrine stable et ce dernier fait est due à la crise des visions du monde). Il n'en reste pas moins que l'on peut également – et parallèlement - constater une reprise de l'ancienne fonction de *l'exemplum* comme illustration d'une doctrine, doctrine qui développe très souvent la bonne conduite à tenir concernant les relations amoureuses (c'est l'argument dont je me suis occupé).[20] Un représentant typique de cette tendance est Giambattista Giraldi Cinzio.[21] Si déjà le commentaire dont le cadre (fuite d'une situation dangereuse créée par le sac de Rome en 1527) entoure chaque nouvelle constitue un garde-fous contre les interprétations aberrantes, les nouvelles sont également farcies de commentaires du narrateur, commentaires qui ont pour fonction d'assurer une communication univoque du message. La nouvelle peut ainsi réassumer la fonction de *l'exemplum*: étayer un système doctrinal. Mais la rigidité des preuves, la sempiternelle surveillance des moindres méandres du récit, montrent bien que l'assurance doctrinale de la Contre-Réforme ne repose pas sur une assiette bien stable: les évidences, les présupposés sont à tout moment sujets au questionnement, et c'est pourquoi ils sont continuellement affirmés, contrairement à des périodes plus sûres de leurs valeurs fondamentales.

Je viens d'évoquer brièvement quelques idées qui ont inspiré mes recherches. J'avais promis de développer mes réflexions dans le sens que je viens d'esquisser, mais, d'une part, pourquoi développer une recherche qui date déjà? D'autre part, le développement esquissé de l'argumentation narrative semble indiquer que, s'il est vrai que la polémique contre les roturiers se fait sentir dans le roman courtois, disons dès le début du XIIIe siècle, les rapports entre groupes et

---

[20] Même dans certaines nouvelles de *l'Heptaméron*, recueil réputé pour son ouverture d'esprit et par la complexité de la relation cadre-nouvelles, on constate pourtant parfois un contre-courant: une tendance à la 'régression' vers *l'exemplum*: protagonistes-types (mari et femme, le plus souvent) abréviation du récit (dont les circonstances tendent à être résumés plutôt que narrées), et une fonction argumentative qui valorise le couple marié. Cf. aussi Karen Laugesen: *Kærlighed og Ægteskab i Marguerite de Navarre's 'Heptaméron'* 1990 (mémoire rédigé au Centre universitaire de Roskilde, accessible dans sa bibliothèque).

[21] *Gli Hecatommithi* t. I.. Venezia 1566, (1. éd. 1565), Gli *Hecatommithi* t. II.. Venezia 1608, (. éd. 1565).

classes ne commencent à poser des problèmes, dans la nouvelle, que vers les temps de la Renaissance. C'est probablement à cette période que s'opère le durcissement entre groupes et classes qu'on n'est que trop enclin de projeter en arrière sur le Moyen Age. Mais les problèmes du couple ne se limitent pas aux tensions qui ont pu exister entre les groupes sociaux. Je me permets donc d'aborder par un autre biais la problématique de notre congrès.

Après tant d'années passées au service de la sémiotique, je suis devenu curieux du vécu. Or, s'il est vrai que la culture modélise et forme l'individu et son expérience - que serait l'amour sans la culture? - cette formation ne se fait pas sans créer des problèmes, souvent graves. Parfois une réalité à peine thématisée arrive à percer au travers des macro-structures des systèmes culturels.

Comment s'y prendre si l'on veut se faire un idée de ce qu'ont pu être les rapports du couple au Moyen Age? Il ne faudrait certainement pas trop se fier aux nouvelles, et surtout pas aux nouvelles ressortissant à la tradition courtoise. Nous y voyons l'élaboration d'une utopie. Et d'ailleurs le mariage, une fois contracté, ne semble pas inviter au lyrisme (il y a des raisons structurales à cela; je viens de les évoquer).

Présuppositions

Pour reconstituer la réalité, on peut, (mais dans quelle mesure?) essayer d'étudier les présupposés des assertions qu'on trouve dans les textes littéraires. Quant on voit louer la propreté (des nappes, des lits, des habits, etc.) on ne court guère de risque à en conclure que la saleté était un phénomène répandu (de nos jours on provoquerait au moins l'étonnement à dire, sans motif particulier, qu'une personne est propre et bien lavée).

On peut donc hésiter, quand on lit les grosses articulations d'un récit médiéval: pour prendre maintenant un exemple qui concerne le thème de ce congrès, nous voyons souvent, dans le premier roman courtois (Chrétien de Troyes, Gautier d'Arras, Jean Renard) le mariage entre nobles riches et pauvres. Un Erich Köhler a interprété cet élément structural du récit, comme une idéologie qui a pour fonction de contribuer à la cohésion de la noblesse devant une royauté qui se fait toujours plus menaçante pour les féodaux.

Une telle interprétation, indépendamment de sa valeur de vérité, ne va pas de soi: elle s'appuie sur des études historiques de la période étudiée.

Un motif tel que la conversation au lit entre mari et femme pourrait être un correctif aux valeurs que l'on ne lit que trop facilement à la surface des récits:

antiféminisme latent mais, également, adoration de la dame lointaine. Probablement le lit, lieu du sommeil, de la procréation et de la mort, était aussi un des
rares endroits où mari et femme pouvaient - à voix basse, car il pouvait y avoir
des serviteurs dans la chambre - échanger des confidences. C'est au lit que la
duchesse de *La Dame de Vergy* amène son mari à lui communiquer le secret de
l'amour du jeune chevalier, ce qui provoquera la catastrophe. C'est également au
lit qu'Énide raconte à Érec ce que les gens disent de lui. Chrétien de Troyes
évoque brièvement, comme antécédent de leur conversation, les ébats amoureux
entre les époux, mais, comme je viens de le dire, le roman courtois tâche
d'intégrer l'amour dans le mariage. C'est au lit que, dans *Le Réconfort de
Madame du Fresne* d'Antoine de la Salle, madame du Chastel encourage son
mari à préférer son honneur à la vie de leur fils, donné comme otage. Ces
exemples montrent que mari et femme ont pu avoir des rapports de confiance
(dans un cas la confiance n'est pas justifiée, néanmoins elle est présupposée).
Or ces rapports ne sont pas souvent développés directement dans les textes.

L'analyse des présuppositions peut d'ailleurs contribuer également à modifier
ce qu'a de trop absolu la simplification qui veut que l'amour- passion ne puisse
pas exister entre mari et femme. Un seul exemple: quand dans le *Filocolo* (II,
72-73) de Boccace, Cressida se demande si elle doit accepter de devenir la
maîtresse de Troilo. La possibilité de l'épouser (ce qui sauvegarderait la décence)
se présente aussitôt à son esprit. Elle écarte l'alternative, car un mari qu'on
aurait toujours à ses côtés, diminuerait l'amour (qui vit de difficulté et de
séparation). Néanmoins le présupposé de cette réflexion établit un rapport entre
l'amour et le mariage.[22]

Finalement, à condition de réfléchir sur quelques exemples de réalisations
érotiques, telles que les décrivent certaines nouvelles, on se rend compte que les
rapports extramatrimoniaux ont dû être, non seulement dangereux (ce qui fait
appel au romanesque) mais également mal commodes. Ce n'est donc pas un
hasard si Boccace accorde le plus souvent, toute la nuit, voire des semaines et
des mois à ses amants. Cela n'allait pas de soi. Souvent seule la présentation
littéraire rend appétissantes des aventures qui, à les supposer réalisables, ont dû
être expédiées à la diable et dans un état de peur permanent.

Nouvelles 'populaires'

Si l'on se méfie de l'idéalisation du couple faite dans la tradition courtoise, on
pourrait également se tourner vers quelques recueils de nouvelles qui échappent

---

[22] Cf. G. Boccaccio: *Tutte le opere* II, éd. V. Branca, Mondadori 1964, p. 61 s.

à cette tradition. Il existe des recueils de nouvelles, dont quelques-unes situées dans le Moyen Age, qui projettent une tout autre lumière sur le couple que les recueils d'inspiration aristocratique. Sans avoir accès à la réalité telle quelle, on la voit pourtant sous un éclairage bien différent.

Qu'est-ce qui oppose les récits d'amour appartenant au domaine courtois à la nouvelle et, de façon plus générale, aux récits que j'ai appelés populaires,[23] et pour lesquelles le terme de non-courtois con- viendrait peut-être mieux? Je vous ferai tout simplement part de quelques observations, sans prétendre à une définition quelconque de la nouvelle populaire ou non-courtoise.

A titre indicatif, je citerai quelques exemples. Au domaine courtois ressortent: *Le Décaméron* de Boccace, *Il Pecorone* de Ser Giovanni,[24] *Il novellino* de Masuccio salernitano[25] et, plus tard, *Le Porretane* de Sabadino degli Arienti.[26]

Au domaine non courtois appartiennent *Il Trecentonovelle* de Franco Sacchetti,[27] *Le Novelle* de Sercambi, *Les Cent Nouvelles Nouvelles*[28] par certains de ses aspects, et plus tard *Le Grand Parangon de Nouvelles* de Nicolas de Troyes.[29]

Mais comment cerner le champs de la nouvelle non-courtoise? Tout au plus, une première approche fournira, non pas une définition, mais tout au plus la description d'une famille, telle la célèbre définition des 'jeux' que donne Wittgenstein.[30]

Tout d'abord, si l'extraction sociale des auteurs et le public auquel ces nouvelles sont destinées ne sont pas sans importance (quelques auteurs sont de culture non-aristocratique, d'autres, des presque inconnus, le sont probablement[31]) il existe des nouvelles de forme populaire, mais appartenant à un

---

23 Dans Les *Transformations* ... pp. 278 ss. et *Amore*... pp. 158 ss.

24 Ser Giovanni: *Il Pecorone*, éd. Enzo Esposito. Longo editore, Ravenna 1974.

25 Masuccio salernitano: *Il Novellino*, éd. G. Petrocchi, Firenze 1957, reprint 1975, éd. Salvatore S. Nigro 1957.

26 Giovanni Sabadino degli Arienti: *Le Porretane*, éd. P. Stoppelli. Japadre editore, L'Aquila 1975 et Giovanni Sabadino degli Arienti: *Le Porretane*, éd. Bruno Basile. I Novellieri Italiani vol. 13. Salerno editrice, Roma. 1981.

27 Franco Sacchetti: "Il Trecentonovelle". *Opere*, éd. A. Borlenghi.Riz zoli, Milano 1957.

28 Anom.: *Les Cent Nouvelles Nouvelles. Conteurs français du XIIe siècle*, éd. Pierre Jourda. Éd. de la pléiade, Gallimard, Paris. 1965.

29 Nicolas de Troyes: *Le Grand Parangon des Nouvelles Nouvelles* (Choix), éd. Krystyna Kasprzyk. Paris 1970.

30 Ludwig Wittgenstein: *Philosophische Untersuchungen/Philosophical Investigations*. Basil Blackwell, Oxford 1953, pp. 31 ss.

31 Ainsi, sur Straparola, nous ne savons à peu près rien.

milieu courtois. Tel est le cas de certains *fabliaux* (une minorité), si l'analyse de
Nykrog est correcte,[32] et celui des *Cent Nouvelles nouvelles*, provenant des
milieux de la cour de Bourgogne et dont l'ironie est plus anti-courtoise que non
courtoise. Le peuple lui-aussi devient chez les aristocrates un concept idéologique, donnant lieu à certains scénarios stéréotypés, tout comme le peuple
charge les images qu'il se fait des princes et de la noblesse.

Mais tentons une première caractéristique interne des textes:

1º Dans le domaine courtois, l'action est présentée comme un événement
unique;[33] Dans le domaine non-courtois, par contre, l'action tend vers *l'itérativité*. Si l'action elle-même est unique, elle tend néanmoins à être explicitement
un exemple de quelque chose qui se passe souvent, ainsi par exemple l'insatiabilité des femmes. On raconte sur l'arrière-fond de la sagesse des nations des
événements qui exemplifient celle-ci, (pour rappel de mémoire, dirait-on).

2º Dans le domaine courtois, le récit offre aux lecteurs de fortes possibilités
d'identification à un ou plusieurs des personnages; dans la nouvelle populaire,
la distance par rapport aux événements narrés est plus grande. Cela a une grande
importance pour les questions du couple et de l'amour. Dans un cas, nous
poursuivons avec les protagonistes une utopie (qui s'alimente de nos propres
rêves), dans l'autre, nous gardons une certaine distance, parfois pour observer
quelque chose d'incompréhensible ou d'obsédant. Il est vrai que le sourire d'un
Boccace ne permet pas une identification totale. L'ironie, souvent aimable, de
l'auteur, porte pourtant rarement atteinte aux possibilités d'identification (et dans
la tradition courtoise de la nouvelle, cette ironie envers des amants bien nés tend
à disparaître, (sauf dans *l'Heptaméron*, où elle tourne à l'amertume). L'ironie
"populaire", si elle est plus lourde (ce que l'on se complaît à répéter), est surtout
créatrice de distance.

Il ne s'agit évidemment que de tendances. Une exception notable est l'introduction du conte de fées (défini par le modèle proppien[34]), qui fait fortement
appel à l'identification avec le héros. Elle a lieu dans des recueils populaires: on
trouve quatre exemples dans les *Novelle* de Sercambi,[35] et avec *Le piacevoli
notti* de Straparola ce genre prend son essor.[36] Le besoin de rêve des couches

---

32   Per Nykrog: *Les Fabliaux*, Munksgaard, Copenhague – Droz, Genève 1957, 1973 (avec
      postface de l'auteur).

33   Boccace insiste sur l'unicité de l'événement (fictif bien entendu) qu'il narre.

34   Vladimir Propp: *Morphologie du conte*. Seuil, Points, Paris 1970 (1965).

35   Je cite d'après Giovanni Sercambi: *Novelle*, éd. Giovanni Sinicropi, Laterza, Bari 1972.
      Cf. aussi Giovanni Sercambi: *Il Novelliere*, éd. Luciano Rossi, Salerno editrice, Roma
      1974.

moyennes trouvent sa réalisation dans l'utopie féerique, dans un monde radicalement coupé du monde du lecteur.[37]

3° Ainsi le domaine courtois présente, au niveau des valeurs, de *fortes transformations des valeurs* (l'amour souvent caractérisé de façon plus spécifique, est affirmé ou nié) alors que, dans les nouvelles non-courtoises, les valeurs sont pour ainsi dire données d'avance. On raconte quand-même, et les raison de ces récits doivent souvent se chercher dans l'acceptation désabusée de la sagesse des nations à travers le gros rire.

Dans ce sens, l'étude du 'motto' serait prometteur. Beaucoup de choses justes ont été avancés sur le 'motto':[38] dans la nouvelle aristocratique, sa fonction peut être le seul recours laissé au socialement faible devant le plus fort; parfois, le 'motto' va jusqu'à rappeler, préciser subtilement, ou transformer les normes de la société (la VIe journée du *Décaméron* en donne de bons exemples). Dans la nouvelle non-courtoise par contre, le destinataire semble souvent se trouver au même niveau que le narrateur. On y trouve donc la sempiternelle affirmation de préjugés; ainsi par exemple, dans certaines sentences que Sercambi attribue à la légendaire Monna Bambacia, une jeune mariée est très active pendant sa première nuit passée avec son mari. Celui-ci se plaint devant Monna Bambacia de ce qu'elle pourrait bien n'être pas vierge. Celle-ci remet en liberté un jeune caneton, qui se dirige tout de suite vers l'eau: tout comme le caneton cherche l'eau, la nature de la femme lui commande de chercher le plaisir.[39]

4° Les recueils de nouvelles 'populaires' n'actualisent pas trop les oppositions de rangs et de classes.[40] Comme je viens de le dire, la presque seule et notable exception parmi les recueils d'inspiration courtoise est le *Décaméron*.[41]

J'ai déjà rappelé que, dans la nouvelle non courtoise, l'on ne saisira pas une image directe du couple du Moyen Age. Mais ces récits offriront du moins une

---

36 Giovan Francesco Straparola: *Le Piacevoli Notti* I-II, éd. G. Rua. Laterza, Bari 1927.

37 Évidemment la nouvelle populaire n'a nullement besoin de s'adresser au bas peuple. Reste que dans le conte de fées la haute noblesse (et surtout les rois) sont décrits d'une manière stéréotypée qui montre que cette littérature ne s'adresse nullement à des courtisans.

38 André Rochon: *Formes et significations de la "beffa" dans la littérature italienne de la Renaissance*. Centre de recherche sur la Renaissance italienne I Université de la Sorbonne nouvelle, Paris 1972.

39 Nouvelle *57*.

40 Excepté le mépris pour les paysans qu'il partagent avec la presque totalité des autres recueils.

41 En ce qui concerne la nouvelle courtoise, on peut d'ailleurs se demander si la polémique narrative contre les classes inférieures appartient à un niveau explicite ou si elle appartient aux présupposés du récit. Il semble qu'entre les différents recueils il existe sur ce point des différences intéressantes.

image autre. Il se peut que les traits qui distinguent la nouvelle populaire laisseront effectivement passer plus de l'expérience quotidienne vécue.

J'ai l'impression que le réel est pour ainsi dire cité, cité pour être condamné ou bien accepté sans trop d'illusions (cette alternative ouvre un choix selon le caractère des auteurs, leur vision du monde etc.). Quoi qu'il en soit, pour la nouvelle populaire, le réel est présenté comme presque impossible à modifier. La création d'un *monde possible* utopique (sauf alors féerique: sans lien, ou presque, avec le monde quotidien) n'est pas du domaine de la nouvelle populaire.

Sercambi

Le couple dans la nouvelle populaire constituerait un champ bien trop vaste. D'ailleurs les problèmes du couple ont pu se poser de façon bien différente au Moyen Age, selon les périodes et les pays différents. J'ai donc préféré me pencher, pendant le temps qui me reste, sur un cas précis: le *Novelle* de Giovanni Sercambi.

Sercambi écrit ses nouvelles autour de l'an 1400. Il joua par ailleurs un rôle politique important à Lucques comme partisan de la *signoria* de Paul Guinigi, et ses *Croniche* constituent une des sources les plus impor- tantes pour l'histoire de son temps.[42]

Il peut être d'un certain intérêt d'essayer de déterminer l'extraction sociale de l'auteur qui va nous occuper, ainsi que son idéologie.

L'appartenance sociale de Sercambi. Son idéologie

L'appartenance politique de Sercambi peut être assez difficile à déterminer. L'unanimité règne sur quelques faits:

1º: l'auteur des *Croniche* fut fauteur de *signoria* (celle de Paolo Guinigi, instaurée en 1400) et il fut donc l'expression d'une idéologie autoritaire.

C'est d'ailleurs ce qui se voit directement de la structure de nouvelles: nombreux sont les récits qui approuvent narrativement l'exercice de l'autorité[43]

---

[42] Giovanni Sercambi: *Le Croniche*, éd. Salvatore Bongi, Giusti, Lucca 1892.

[43] J'ai analysé comparativement le motif de la jeune fille violée et du violateur puni. La nouvelle 6 de Sercambi insiste sur la nécessité de punir, rien que pour affirmer l'autorité du prince, cf. "L'Analisi narrativa della novella rinascimentale? Variazioni sul tema della riparazione dello stupro." *Mémoires de la Société Néophilologique de Helsinki, publiés sous la direction de Tauno F. Mustanoja.* Tome XLIV. *Actes du 9e Congrès des roma-*

et le cadre substitue à la brigade paritaire du *Décaméron* une troupe donc la plupart des membres sont anonymes et d'où surgissent surtout un 'preposto' (donc un 'chef') et un auteur. Ce narrateur (narrateur unique, contrairement aux dix narrateurs du *Décaméron*) est aussi, dans une poésie acrostique, identifié à la personne de Sercambi. Dans la terminologie d'un Genette, nous sommes donc en présence d'un auteur intradiégétique.[44]

2º: Sercambi fut un parvenu. Il acquit une fortune considérable, mais son père, apothicaire, comme lui-même, n'appartenait pas à l'oligarchie de la ville.

3º Sa culture, bonne, si l'on la place dans un milieu communal,[45] n'avait rien de nouveau. Il fut un homme encore médiéval, expression d'une culture communale.

Mais après cet accord, les avis sur Sercambi diffèrent, aussi bien en ce qui concerne sa religiosité que pour son appartenance politique. Cardini estime que sa religiosité était somme toute assez conformiste,[46] alors que Dornetti, se penchant sur le mouvement des 'Bianchi', pense que Sercambi, sympathiseur de ce mouvement, pourrait friser l'hérésie.[47] Tout au contraire, pour Giuseppe Chiecchi,[48] qui épouse sur ce point les opinions de Rossi, Sercambi est l'expression du moralisme croissant dans le 'popolo grasso' qui, en temps de crise sociale, aurait été alarmé par les couches populaires.[49]

En ce qui concerne les prises de position politiques, Rossi, dans son introduction, estime que le putchiste lucquois serait l'allié du peuple gras et qu'il aurait trahi les intérêts de son propre parti, ceux du menu peuple.[50]

D'autre part, on trouve un Sercambi 'populiste' chez Bongi (éditeur des *Croniche*[51]) et plus tôt chez Tommasi,[52] Minutoli (équitable envers Paolo

---

nistes scandinaves. *Helsinki 13-17 août 1984* pp.285-93 1986, et "Novella e Anticultura. Considerazioni sopra l'analisi della novella". *Rinascimento meridionale e altri studi. Raccolta di studi pubblicata in onore di Mario Santoro*. Società editrice napoletana. pp. 349-59 1987.

44 Gérard Genette: *Figures II* . Seuil, Paris 1969.

45 R. Cardini: "Le "novelle magiche" di Giovanni Sercambi, superstizioni cittadine e superstizioni rurali in uno scrittore "borghese" del Trecento toscano". *Ricerche storiche IV* pp. 169-241 1974.

46 "Le "novelle magiche"... p. 182s.

47 V. Dornetti: "Le novelle di Giovanni Sercambi e il moralismo dei Bianchi". *Italianistica 8* pp. 275-296 1979.

48 Giuseppe Chiecchi: "Sulla moralità di Giovanni Sercambi!. *Lettere italiane 29* pp. 133-147 1977.

49 Chiecchi p. 134, Rossi 1971.

50 P. LXIV.

Guinigi)[53] et Cianelli[54] qui, tout en chantant les louanges de Paolo Guinigi, le décrit (citant Sercambi) comme plébiscité par le peuple (p. 188 s.) et insiste sur sa bienfaisance envers le menu peuple (p. 128). Dinucci,[55] écrivant sous le fascisme naissant, comprend Sercambi (et Paolo Guinigi) comme des défenseur de la patrie. Il raille les historiens lucquois qui, vivant sous une oligarchie "che aveva sembiante di libero reggimento," ne sauraient comprendre un homme comme Sercambi qui donna sa patrie au pouvoir d'une seule famille puissante.

Je me suis plutôt rattaché à cette dernière manière de voir. En effet, j'ai écrit que l'idéologie de Sercambi aurait appartenu à la petite bourgeoisie.[56] Il semble me aussi que Dornetti et Salwa[57] considèrent plutôt notre auteur comme un esprit populaire.

Passons brièvement en revue les différentes possibilités:

1º Sercambi a pu, tout en gardant un éventuel esprit petitbourgeois de sa jeunesse devenir l'allié de la grande bourgeoisie. Ce point de vue se concilie facilement avec son tout aussi hypotéthique arrivisme (nous savons qu'il est 'arrivé' et non pas qu'il était arriviste); cela reviendrait à faire un procès d'intentions, voire de juger un homme du bas Moyen Age sur ses opinions, chose qui de nos jours revêt une grande importance, (du moins en polémique),

---

51   Giovanni Sercambi: *Le Croniche*, éd. Salvatore Bongi, Giusti, Lucca 1992, note au chap. 347, p. 452.

52   Giro Iamo Tommasi: Cf. *Sommario della storia di Lucca dall'anno MIV all'anno MDCC...* continuato sino all'anno 1799 ... per cura di Carlo Minutoli. Vieusseux, Firenze 1847.

53   Carlo Minutoli: "Intorno la vita e gli scritti di Giovanni Sercambi". *Atti della R. Accademia dei Filomati degli anni 1844-45 offerti a sua altezza reale Carlo Locovico duca di Lucca.* Giusti Lucca 1845.

54   A.N. Cianelli: *Memorie e documenti per servire all'istoria della città e stato di Lucca* tomo II.. Francesco Bertini, Lucca 1812.

55   Alberto Guglielmo Dinucci: "Giovanni Sercambi e le sue cronache". *Rassegna nazionale.* 2. serie. Vol LVII pp. 43-103 1927.

56   *Amore* ... pp. 103 note, où d'ailleurs j'ai trop sollicité le texte d'Augusto Mancini: *Storia di Lucca.* Sansoni Firenze 1950 p. 170. A l'endroit cité, cet auteur n'affirme pas que les Guinigi avaient l'appui du menu peuple, mais seulement qu'il étaient contre les magnates, pour un gouvernement 'a popolo', donc, grosso modo, 'républicain'.

57   Cf. Dornetti: "Le novelle de G. S.... et Piotr Salwa: "Sercambi e Boccaccio: Problemi e prospettive". Kwartalnik Neofilologicny T. XXX, nr. 2 1983, "Retorica e politica – *Croniche e novelle* di Giovanni Sercambi, lucchese." *Renaissance Studies in Honor of Craig Hugh Smyth* 1985, "*Fiction* e realtà. Novella come fonte storica". *I Tatti Studies. Essays in the Renaissance.* Vol. *I* 1985, "Il novelliere'di Sercambi tra il comico e il serio". *Kwartalnik Neofilologicny* T. XXXII, nr. 2 1985, "Il mito di Roma nelle novelle di Giovanni Sercambi". *Testo n. 11* 1986.

mais qui aux jours de Sercambi le cédait, encore plus que maintenant, aux solidarités concrètes.

2º Sercambi a pu garder sa solidarité avec le menu peuple, adoptant l'attitude 'césariste': une alliance entre les seigneurs et le menu peuple (contre la bourgeoisie d'affaires) n'était pas chose nouvelle (pensons au duc d'Athènes qui, à Florence, un demi siècle auparavant s'était appuyé, aussi, sur le menu peuple auquel il accorda après sa prise de pouvoir le droit de former deux 'artes', dont l''arte' des teinturiers, particulièrement mal vu par les fabricants de laine).

3º Or, d'après les ouvrages récents, que j'aurais dû mettre à profit plus tôt, la lutte pour le pouvoir à Lucca entre les Guinigi et les Forteguerra, ne semble pas avoir revêtu la forme d'une lutte entre classes, ni même celle entre groupes sociaux. Les Forteguerra et les Guinigi représentent, tous les deux, la bourgeoisie et il est bien difficile de noter des différences importantes dans la composition des deux factions.[58] La noblesse – déjà écartée du pouvoir par le statut de 1308, bien plus radical que *gli Ordinamenti di Giustizia* de Florence,[59] avait de nouveau été émarginée – et cela de façon bien plus radicale qu'à Florence, dès 1370 (une année après l'indépendance reconquise)[60] et le *popolo minuto*, sans être formellement exclu de l'exercice du pouvoir, y participa bien peu pendant la période qui nous intéresse.[61]

Tout au plus peut-on constater que parmi les partisans des Guinigi figure un nombre non négligeable d'artisans et d'hommes inconnus. Auraient-ils de ce fait été le parti des petites gens et des arrivistes? Cela n'est même pas sûr. Toujours selon Meek, il pourrait s'agir d'une illusion d'optique: les listes des partisans des Guinigi sont tout simplement de beaucoup plus longues que celles des partisans des Forteguerra[62] (et les Guinigi, et non les Forteguerra furent en état de récompenser leurs fidèles).

Il semble donc bien que le combat cesse faute de combattants. Si il n'y avait

---

[58] Cf.Ch. Meek: *Lucca 1369-1400, Politics and Society in an Early Renaissance City-State.* Oxford UP 1978, p. 223.

[59] Cf. Louis Green: "Society and Politics in fourteenth Century Lucca" . *Altro Polo*, éd. Condren C. & Pesman Cooper, R. Univ. of Sydney 1982, p. 31. L'article de Green est une excellent mise à point de la situation politique de Lucques. Selon cet auteur, après la "tyrannie" des Guinigi, Lucques trouva une assiette stable sous forme d'oligarchie républicaine.

[60] Meek pp. 182 ss.

[61] Cf. Meek pp. 181, 185 ss. et A. Romiti: "La classe politica lucchese nei primi anni di libertà". *Archivio storico italiano* Anno CXL 1982.

[62] Cf. Meek pp. 205 ss. et 225.

pas de lutte de classes, mais des luttes de factions, il est oiseux de continuer ces débats.

Il faut d'ailleurs se rappeler qu'à ma connaissance, les débats ont été ouvert par des partisans du républicanisme oligarchique de Lucques (qui a duré jusque l'intervention de Napoléon). Ce sont les républicains conservateurs qui ont reproché aux Guinigi et, partant, à Sercambi, d'avoir fait appel aux couches populaires. Tommasi, Minutoli, Bongi et, plus favorable au populaire, Dinucci. Quant au faits – des couches populaires semblent effectivement avoir pris part aux troubles en 1392 et en 1400 – ils ne demandent guère d'explications, tant l'habitude d'avoir recours à la rue était courante. Il reste néanmoins curieux que Bongi, dans la personne d'un "Andrea cantatore" ait pu identifier un ancien participant au tumulte des Ciompi.[63]

Que Sercambi ait été bourgeois ou petit-bourgeois peut être difficile à déterminer. Il termina sa vie dans une aisance économique et jamais il ne fut pauvre, mais, d'autre part, j'ai quelque difficulté à attribuer à un fils d'apothicaire, une origine de grand bourgeois.

Si l'on veut définir l'appartenance de classe d'un écrivain il faut opérer plusieurs *distinguo*. Tout d'abord celui entre l'homme et l'écrivain, distinction qui s'impose a fortiori pour qui comme Sercambi participa activement à la vie politique de sa ville.

L'humus dont s'inspire une oeuvre littéraire est souvent celui de l'enfance et de la première jeunesse. On change assez facilement d'idées et l'on peut changer de parti politique. Il est plus difficile de changer l'appartenance fondamentale, de changer les attitudes, valeurs et manières de voir dans lesquelles on a baignée dès la première enfance. Par manque d'information, il ne nous est guère possible de décrire la première socialisation du petit Giovanni (comme un Sartre a pu l'essayer pour Flaubert). Même l'enfance d'un Boccace, un peu mieux connu, ne fournit pas d'éléments pour constituer une image de *l'homme*, abstraction faite de l'oeuvre.

Pour déterminer la vision du monde de Sercambi, le plus sûr sera donc de se tourner tout simplement vers l'oeuvre.

Les Novelle

Les *Novelle* de Sercambi parlent abondamment de l'amour, elles donnent des détails crus et précis mais, comme le note finement Christian Bec,[64] elles sont

---

[63] Cf. *Croniche* I chap. 346-48 et note au chap. 347, p. 452.

presque sans érotisme n'offrant ainsi pas de possibilité d'identification au lecteur. La fatigue et le dégoût de l'acte sexuel, qui existent aussi, mais sous forme voilée dans la tradition courtoise tardive ou sous forme présupposée, dans certains contes à rire, sont, chez Sercambi, souvent lourdement étalés. Cela vaut pour l'insatiabilité de la femme, topos connu, qui sert dans les Cent *Nouvelles Nouvelles* ou dans le *Grand Parangon Des Nouvelles Nouvelles*, à donner une fin spirituelle à un récit ou à poser plaisamment un problème à résoudre, voire comme simple présupposé d'un mot d'esprit. Chez Sercambi, cette insatiabilité est affirmée à toute occasion qui s'offre, et elle l'emporte même les rares fois qu'un code courtois a été évoqué pour décrire le commencement d'un amour.[65]

Le Monde de Sercambi

La culture de Sercambi, qui est réelle, est aussi assez limitée. Il n'a probablement guère voyagé dans sa jeunesse, il ne s'est pas longuement imbu, tel Boccace, d'une culture courtoise ou humaniste. On peut donc avancer, sans trop de risques, que son substrat culturel est celui de la ville de Lucques, sans de grandes perspectives sur d'autres cultures.

Cela n'empêche nullement que Sercambi ne connaisse des sites autres que Lucques. Reste à savoir quelles sont les sources des descriptions de Sercambi, quel est son réalisme. Or les éditeurs Sinicropi et Rossi voient dans le *Dittamondo* de Fazio degli Uberti une source importante des connaissances géographiques de Sercambi. Ses sources seraient donc en grande partie livresques et probablement, ce qui est plus important, à ce monde il manque l'élément fabuleux, le rêve. Alors qu'un Boccace peut étendre l'effet de réel jusqu'aux régions orientales ou légendaires où parfois il campe ses personnages, régions qu'il réussit à rattacher à la réalité quotidienne italienne, je ne ressens aucun "effet de réel" en lisant les décors où Sercambi place les siens: son réel est d'une autre nature.

A y regarder de plus près, il ne manque pourtant nullement a Sercambi des notations précises, et d'autant plus précises que l'on se rapproche de la région de Lucques. Tout est soigneusement localisé. Bec a signalé que presque toutes

---

64 Cf. Ch. Bec: *Les Marchands écrivains à Florence 1375-1434*. Mouton La Haye – Paris 1967, pp. 175-198.

65 Cf. nouvelle *55 Une jeune fille déclare noblement son amour à son amant.* L'auteur reprend cet amour par "la rabia indel culo". Il est vrai que la jeune fille, trahissant son père au profit de l'amant, oublie toute loyauté, mais, justement, Sercambi se complaît dans les descriptions des suites catastrophiques de l'amour.

ses nouvelles sont situées non seulement dans l'espace, mais aussi dans le temps.

Mais au fond, pourquoi vouloir expliquer pourquoi un écrivain original à sa manière n'arrive pas à égaler un Boccace?

On pourrait attribuer à Sercambi, à lire ses nouvelles, une certaine mesquinerie. Aucun humour, une peur des voleurs et bandits, une obsession à punir, une obscénité sans érotisme, comme le dit si bien Christian Bec. Reste à savoir à qui attribuer ses traits? En jargon: s'agit-il d'un sociolecte ou bien d'un idéolecte? Il peut, évidemment, y avoir un chevauchement entre les deux termes. On ne peut pas exclure que la grande bourgeoisie d'affaires ne soit apeurée (mais alors devant quoi? devant des couches populaires qui, à Lucques, ne bougent pas?). A risquer un parallèle avec les circonstances actuelles je placerais plus volontiers les peurs dans la petite bourgeoisie, qui est souvent le support du victorianisme et d'attitudes rigouristes.

Si Sercambi ne prend certainement pas le parti du bas peuple, l'on constate chez lui peu de sympathie envers les grands (à moins qu'ils ne soient revêtues de fonctions politiques; dans ce cas ils sont évalués selon les mérites de leurs actes). Je choisis, pour les raisons que j'ai avancées, de voir dans les *Novelle* une image précieuse d'une mentalité petite-bourgeoise telle qu'elle a pu exister à Lucques autours de l'an 1400.

Le Système narratif de Sercambi.

J'ai tentativement classé les *Novelle* de Sercambi dans le groupe (encore trop mal défini) des nouvelles populaires.[66] Parcourons donc les critères proposés plus haut en guise de définition pour voir en quelle mesure les nouvelles érotiques de Sercambi s'y conforment.

1º *l'itérativité*? Les nouvelles de Sercambi ne satisfont qu'en partie à ce critère. D'une part, il est vrai qu'elles actualisent un trait que l'on trouve dans la nouvelle populaire: la femme (presque) toujours prête à l'amour. Le désir bestial est placé le plus souvent dans la femme. Ce trait est une telle obsession que l'auteur n'y renonce même pas devant le scénario de la femme violée. Ainsi, même une femme honnête, tenue prisonnière par des soldats qui abusent d'elles, profitent de l'occasion pour satisfaire sans infamie - et encore seulement en partie! – son désir insatiable, quitte à reprendre, après sa libération son rôle de honnête épouse (77). De même, lorsqu'il développe le scénario de la vierge

---

[66] *Amore...*

violée, la nécessité de la punition résulte, non pas de la faute commise envers la jeune fille qui, ayant déjà pris goût à l'amour, se serait contentée d'une somme d'argent ou bien du mariage avec le coupable, mais de la transgression des ordres du prince (6).[67]

Sercambi ne joue même pas sur la différence être-paraître (la femme semblant ou se donnant pour chaste et révélant (corps du récit) sa nature libidineuse). Il ne se complaît pas à établir une limite pour aussitôt la faire transgresser, comme dans certains recueils écrits par et pour des viveurs qui sentent le besoin de faire émoustiller leur désir (le Moyen Age aussi connaît la fameuse crise du désir dont on parle tant).

Ainsi l'"amar a nullo amato amar perdona" est à prendre dans un sens physiologique cru. Aussitôt qu'une femme découvre le désir d'un homme, "celui-là veut me sauter", pense-t-elle, et voilà l'affaire engagée.[68] Ou bien, une abbesse découvre-t-elle une religieuse avec son amant? Elle veut tout de suite sa part et ne constitue même pas au début du récit l'autorité traditionnelle qui devrait et pourrait punir, quitte à y renoncer, soit parce qu'elle est prise en délit de fornication elle-même, soit parce que, aguichée, elle veut sa part de l'aubaine. Bien au contraire, le récit de Sercambi débute par des scènes de masturbation entre religieuses).[69] Ne reste comme thème que le désir qui s'éveille immédiatement. Je cite en note une liste, nullement exhaustive, de nouvelles se terminant mal pour les amants, dans lesquelles les femmes, toujours, sont prêtes.[70] Si l'adultère réussit, Sercambi réduit le succès à l'exemple de la lubricité de la femme et condamne le succès dans les titres ou dans les commentaires d'auteur.[71] A ce premier niveau, Sercambi est plus populaire que les nouvelles populaires, faisant sauter l'être-paraître qui pouvait offrir – ou étayer – la trame d'un récit.

Mais si l'itérativité est de règle, Sercambi n'en argumente pas moins narrativement. Seulement, l'enjeu majeur est placé ailleurs. Sercambi est moraliste et ne tolère guère l'immoralité, mais quelle est sa morale?

Il est vrai que bien des nouvelles sont punitives, mais les punitions de Sercambi ont entre elles une caractéristique particulière: en ce qui concerne les particuliers, la punition c'est bien, la punition secrète, ou bien la punition par le hasard, c'est mieux. Ce trait distingue les nouvelles de Sercambi de celles de la tradition courtoise, ou, si punitions il y a, celles-ci sont affirmées, voire célébrées.

---

[67] Cf. "L'Analisi narrativa della novella ..." et "Novella e Anticultura...."

[68] Nouvelle *138*.

[69] Nouvelle 31.

[70] *5, 9, 13, 14, 15, 32, 51, 55, 83, 96, 111, 116, 119, 127, 133, 138, 142, 143, 150, 152, 154.*

[71] *79, 101, 107, 117, 119, 151, 126.*

Les maris sercambiens se trouvent placés dans un dilemme. Ce dilemme n'est au fond qu'un scénario culturel bien connu: le mari cocufié doit rétablir son honneur, mais Sercambi prend ce dilemme au sérieux. Plus souvent que d'autres nouvellistes, Sercambi envisage les conséquences de la punition, conséquences souvent périlleuses.

Un mari est obligé de punir une femme infidèle. S'il ne le fait pas, il est déshonoré. Dans la nouvelle *154*, d'une grande précision dans les détails érotiques, le mari benêt vante à sa femme, déjà volage, la taille du membre d'un barbier. En se donnant au mari, celle-ci s'imagine déjà entre les bras du barbier, situation qui, bien sûr, se réalise.[72] L'intérêt se porte, encore ici, sur les modalités de la punition. Le mari lâche prise, allant vivre à la campagne avec une prostituée et racontant à tout venant ses malheurs conjugaux, ce dont l'auteur le blâme. Ce sont les parents qui se charge de mutiler le barbier, mais le mari ne reprend pas sa femme.

Mais si le mari tue sa femme, il risque d'être condamné à mort, ainsi dans la nouvelle *116*, qui est raconté comme exemple contre la paresse: le mari aurait dû intervenir plus tôt, avant l'adultère accompli.

Si un mari doit punir, il préfère le faire en secret: "con onesto modo": cela évite les complications: lutte entre deux familles etc.[73] Ainsi, dans la nouvelle 133, un mari punit une fornication en chaîne entre sa femme et ses enfants et un serviteur avec beaucoup de discrétion: le serviteur est assassiné en secret par des parents du mari et c'est seulement plus tard que le mari tue sa femme et ses enfants. De même, dans la nouvelle *152* un gentilhomme arrive à tuer sa femme et son amant, un meunier réputé par ses attributs virils, et cela sans être aperçu par personne. Pour montrer combien est important le secret de la punition, citons un dernier exemple, maladroit, celui-là, mais d'autant plus significatif comme révélateur de ce trait qui s'impose contre toute vraisemblance: Dans la nouvelle *143*, Sercambi reprend une nouvelle du *Décaméron* (*VII,4,* la pierre au puits) avec séquence punitive ajouté. Un détail pris chez Boccace est repris et développé: quand sa femme le prie de lui ouvrir la porte, le mari refuse et l'auteur de commenter: tous les Gênois vont être au courant des affaires du ménage, passage auquel on peut rapprocher la fin de la séquence punitive: le mari tue sa femme sans que personne s'en aperçoive. Ce détail est assez improbable, vu que le mari tue sa femme dans leur maison qui est placée à

---

72 On pourrait parler ici, avec René Girard, de médiation interne. Mais l'implosion des structures narratives menace aussi bien la médiation que l'argumentation narrative.

73 Cf. nouvelles *119* (selon ma lecture cf. *Amore* ... p. 93 s.), *127* (le motif de l'enfant de neige), *152*.

Gênes. Sans beaucoup d'habileté, Sercambi actualise ainsi une de ses obsession: la punition secrète, et du moment que le mari arrive à punir en secret, il est réinvesti de la sympathie de l'auteur.

Rien donc d'étonnant à ce que le mari soit tout heureux d'être débarrassé de la lourde charge qu'est la punition. Ainsi dans la nouvelle qui transforme le motif du "coeur mangé" (cf. la nouvelle *135 = Décaméron IV,9*) où le suicide, tragique chez Boccace, est accueilli par le mari avec joie.

C'est pourquoi Sercambi a souvent recours au hasard. La punition par le hasard, est une action dont l'agent n'est pas un sujet désirant punir ou se venger.

Sercambi arrive même à tourner une nouvelle plaisante en punition. Dans sa version du patenôtre de saint Julien,[74] la bonne fortune est en même temps une punition de l'immoralité de l'amant absent, qui n'est plus un marquis, mais un évêque. Ne passons pas sans signaler qu'ici aussi Sercambi insiste sur la faim érotique permanente de la femme (abolissant ainsi en partie ce qu'a de merveilleux la belle aventure qui se présente).[75]

Le hasard intervient aussi pour venger l'innocence outragée dans les nouvelles *7* et *132* (cette dernière traite le motif du duel, jugement de Dieu, développé dans *Der Zweikampf* de Henrik von Kleist). Rappelons que, contrairement à la peste du *Décaméron*, celle du cadre des *Novelle* est une punition envoyée par Dieu. L'histoire de la chaste Lucrèce est reprise, mentionnant, toutefois sans insister lourdement, que la victime du viol a dû éprouver quelque plaisir (*43*). Ainsi il existe chez Sercambi – mais combien peu! – des femmes chastes.

Qui plus est, les récits sont fortement encadrés. Commentaires et titres, parfois les poésies de Soldanieri citées dans les introductions, sont autant de garde-fous du lecteur et arrivent souvent à infléchir l'interprétation immédiate, plaisante d'un récit érotique. Je ne crois pas que Sercambi soit un hypocrite qui sous voile de moraliste satisfait les appétits égrillards de ses possibles lecteurs. Autre chose est la fascination qu'exercent sur notre Lucquois les choses du sexe, mais on peut être à la fois obsédé et moraliste, voire même jouisseur pervers.

Ainsi Sercambi n'en reste pas à l'itérativité. Il argumente sans aucun doute et l'on observe un retour vers la tradition de l'exemplum, non seulement dans le cadre fortement moralisateur, mais également dans la structure narrative. Avec quelques exceptions notables, Sercambi fait retour à 'l'exemplum deterrens', voire à la structure de la fable antique, décrite par Nøjgaard.[76]

2º *l'identification*? Si par identification, il faut entendre l'identification avec

---

[74] Cf. Décaméron *II,2.*

[75] On trouvera d'autres exemples de punitions par le hasard dans les nouvelles *9, 14, 34, 55*.

[76] Cf. *La Fable antique...*

les amoureux, subsidiairement celle avec l'autorité blessée dans son honneur, les nouvelles n'offrent que peu de possibilités. Comme il est le cas dans la nouvelle populaire, Sercambi n'offre au début du récit que peu de descriptions d'amours naissants, d'instauration de sujets narratifs.[77] Ou plutôt, de par le topos de la femme toujours prête à l'amour, le coup de foudre, fréquent dans la nouvelle courtoise, se réduit à la renommée sexuelle d'un être masculin qui, à cause de la taille de ses attributs virils[78] ou de ses prouesses érotiques, devient par là même objet de désir, du désir d'une femme que le lecteur n'est nullement invité à partager.

Si jamais identification il y a, le sujet proposé est de préférence l'autorité obligée à punir, autorité qui ne punit pourtant pas automatiquement, comme on s'y attendrait (selon le scénario culturel du mari cocu ou menacé de le devenir). En plus, le récit ne propose pas toujours, loin de là, l'exaltation de la punition (et partant, des valeurs rétablies par celle-ci). C'est souvent la lassitude qui domine, ou la joie de la besogne péniblement achevée.

3º *De fortes transformations de valeurs*? La clef que j'ai construite pour établir une description si possible parallèle du niveau des valeurs et des méandres de l'intrigue[79] n'est pas d'une très grande utilité en ce qui concerne les *Novelle*. En cela le recueil Sercambi se conforme à la manière des nouvelles populaires. Il reste pourtant une nuance à faire. Rarement l'amour réussit; le plus souvent l'amour est puni. Mais au fond, les punitions sont peu utiles et n'opèrent pas les transformations de valeurs: la femme, punie ou non, reste insatiable, ne se laisse guère convertir; la cour et la ruse destinées à obtenir le consentement de la femme ont perdu leur objet; les conversions à la vertu sont quasi inexistantes.

On peut ajouter que la preuve narrative consiste souvent en un renvoi dos à dos des conduites présentées. On assiste à un commencement d'implosion des structures narratives, implosion qui n'est guère contrebalancée par la mise en valeur de bons mots.[80] Le résultat de l'action compte peu. Reste la fascination d'une réalité d'une étrange crudité. Si l'on veut parler de transformations, celles-ci consistent dans le rejet de vastes domaines de la réalité.

---

[77] Cf. Algirdas Julien Greimas: "Les Actants, les Acteurs et les Figures". C. Chabrol (éd): *Sémiotique narrative et textuelle*, Larousse, Paris 1973 et A. J. Greimas & J. Courtés: *Sémiotique. dictionnaire raisonné de la théorie du langage..* Hachette, Paris 1979 (sous 'modalité', 'programme narratif' ou 'sujet').

[78] Cf. la nouvelle *79* dans laquelle un jeune homme nommé Cazzutoro s'attire le désir d'une femme, à cause de son nom, ou la nouvelle *152*, déjà évoquée.

[79] Cf. *Transformations...* et *Amore...*

[80] Comme dans les *Facetie* du Pogge ou dans les *Cents Nouvelles Nouvelles*.

4º *Une forte actualisation de l'opposition entre rangs et classes sociales*?

Les *Novelle* semblent se conformer sur ce point aux tendances des nouvelles populaires. A part une distribution classique (certaines nouvelles particulièrement stéréotypées sont placées dans des milieux populaires) le recueil de Sercambi n'argumente pas à base d'appartenance sociale.

Il semble pourtant que l'auteur nourrisse parfois une certaine méfiance envers les couches sociales nobles. Ainsi l'introduction à la nouvelle *117* (reprise du *Décaméron III,4*) approuve moins que Boccace le tour joué au mari qui veut s'anoblir par mariage. Il est plutôt un avertissement à de tels maris sur la malice des femmes de haut rang, attitude qui se trouve confirmé dans la modification du raisonnement de l'homologue de Gualtieri dans la nouvelle *153* qui reprend la nouvelle de Griselda: Le conte Artú (= Gualtieri) se méfie en effet des femmes nobles et de haut rang, désespérant de trouver parmi elles une femme conforme à ses souhaits. D'autre part, et surtout en dehors du domaine de l'amour, on trouve certainement une polémique contre les parias sociaux. Les voleurs qui sont pris au sérieux et donc punis[81] (leurs bons tours ne sont guère acceptés[82]), mais il s'agit d'émarginés qui n'avaient guère de possibilités de faire carrière dans la vie sociale de la cité. L'argumentation de Sercambi ne condamne pas ceux qui voudraient monter l'échelle sociale (elle ne les appuie pas non plus).

L'échec de deux couples
Nouvelle 30

Pour terminer, j'essaierai de serrer de plus près la vision sercambienne du couple. J'examinerai deux nouvelles qui décrivent une recherche de liaison ou de mariage et qui sont toutes deux couronnées par un échec cuisant. Tout d'abord je donnerai un premier résumé de la nouvelle 30, dans lequel j'omets caractérisations (psychologiques et sociales) et évaluations, donc aussi le titre.

Antonia, une dame de Pistoia, emmène un Ricciardo, qui est gravement malade, à une propriété de campagne qu'elle possède. Chemin faisant, Ricciardo lui montre ses bijoux et les lui donne à garder. Puis il lui propose le mariage et une fois arrivé à destination il lui demande de consommer ce mariage tout de suite. Elle exige une promesse de mariage faite dans une église – mais entre eux deux seuls – puis le mariage est réalisé.

---

[81] Cf. *Amore...* p.98 et les nouvelles *19-23, 80, 84, 85, 87-92, 106, 112, 147.*

[82] Cf. nouvelle *19.*

Une fois son désir satisfait, Ricciardo prétend devoir rentrer à Pistoia sous prétexte d'arranger la cérémonie du mariage[83] et, pour ce faire, il a besoin des bijoux qu'Antonia lui rend. Une fois échappé, il se vante de sa bonne aventure. La dame perd sa réputation, elle cite devant l'évêque Ricciardo qui ne nie nullement avoir possédé Antonia "comme on possède les prostituées", mais qui dit qu'il n'a jamais eu l'intention de l'épouser. Antonia est déshonorée et ne regagne jamais son honneur.

Dans un épilogue narratif, épilogues caractéristiques pour Sercambi, on nous raconte que Ricciardo prend femme, mais que celle-ci refuse de le suivre dans un exil et que cette femme subit ce qui fut fait à Antonia (probablement elle est 'possédée' par un autre homme).

Narrativement on constate la double négation que j'ai évoqué: deux échecs: Antonia ne réussit pas à se faire épouser; d'autre part, Ricciardo est puni par le hasard (par l'infidélité de sa femme). Le titre est "De Inganno" (de la tromperie), mais aucune valorisation positive n'est faite d'Antonia. Pourtant, l'auteur la considère bien comme la femme de Ricciardo (puisque la femme infidèle est appelée la seconde femme de Ricciardo).

Une première remarque est à faire: la possibilité d'identification (ne fût-elle que partielle) avec un(e) protagoniste positif est refusé au lecteur. On nous raconte un double exemple, dans lequel les deux personnages sont évalués négativement par deux actions évaluatrices: Antonia est déshonorée, Ricciardo devient cocu (et, partant, déshonoré lui aussi!).

Dans le corpus de nouvelles aristocratiques, on pourrait récrire cette nouvelle comme un bon tour: la sympathie serait investie sur l'homme qui se procurerait un bonne fortune. Comme on le verra, Sercambi fournit déjà les éléments pour une telle réécriture. On pourrait aussi penser à un autre type qui nous est familier à nous autres modernes: la p'tite phâme séduite et abandonnée.[84]

Regardons maintenant les qualifications. Antonia est veuve, probablement elle a passé l'âge d'avoir des enfants, et Ricciardo est jeune. Si Antonia n'est pas pauvre, Ricciardo est beaucoup plus riche qu'elle et il est noble. Antonia

---

83 Georges Duby: *Le chevalier, la femme et le prêtre. Le mariage dans la France féodale.* Hachette, Paris 1978.

84 Mais de quand date précisément ce type? Me vient à l'esprit tout d'abord *Eugénie* de Beaumarchais (qui reprend le motif du mariage simulé, avec la différence qu'aux temps de Sercambi, avant le Concile de Trente,la promesse et l'accomplissement constituaient le mariage). Mais sauf à prolonger, à l'instar de Le Goff le Moyen Age jusqu'à la Révolution Française, on ne saurait dire que ce type appartient au Moyen Age. A ma connaissance, les pauvres filles et femmes victimes, sont toutes forcées, voire violées. Médiévistes aidez-moi!

commet donc – au moins – deux fautes: elle ne tient pas compte des différences sociales (j'y reviendrai tout à l'heure) et elle oublie probablement aussi la fonction du mariage qui est d'avoir des enfants (cette fin est souvent passée sous silence dans la littérature aristocratique, qui décrit le mariage comme le couronnement de l'amour).

Mais qu'en est-il de l'amour? Il se trouve réduit – passez-moi le terme – à "la rage au cul". On pourrait donc penser qu'Antonia ne domine pas ses émois naturels. Est-elle punie pour se laisser emporter par ses instincts? Mais quelle est l'origine de cette rage? Peut- être pas tellement, comme on pourrait le penser, ces instincts, mais bien autre chose.

Arrivé à cet endroit, je demande à mes collègues, mes semblables, mes frères, un effort de sincérité supplémentaire. Qui ne s'est épris d'un(e) partenaire ayant pignon sur rue, possédant de beaux meubles confortables, servant des mets succulents?[85] Forts de ces réflexions, nous pouvons tenter de percer les arcanes de l'amour sercambien. La rage (ou le prurit, comme dit le texte la première fois) est probablement provoqué par les richesses de Ricciardo, richesses dont les bijoux montrés servent de preuves, et le topos de l'insatiabilité sexuelle de la femme, en cache une autre: le désir sexuel socialisé par le désir de la promotion sociale.

L'ultime erreur d'Antonia est de se dessaisir des bijoux de Ricciardo donnés en gage, comprend-on. Elle aussi cherche à tromper, mais c'est ici le mâle qui l'emporte, et elle est condamnée pour n'avoir pas réussi. Nous pouvons ainsi constater une morale de l'effet et non pas une morale des intentions. Comme dans la fable, c'est en dernière instance l'échec qui condamne une conduite (l'action exemplaire). Mais comme je viens de le dire, le trompeur est à son tour trompé.

Nouvelle 18

Une autre nouvelle suffira pour illustrer cette mentalité. Il s'agit de la nouvelle 18, "*De periculo in amore* di Checca delli Asini figliuola di Asinino, vedua bella."

Monna Checca, une veuve, prend un amant. La nouvelle insiste sur les nombreuses difficultés qu'a le couple pour arriver à se rencontrer en secret. Les rencontres dans les jardins sont souvent empêchées par les intempéries. Une rencontre dans un couvent, dans lequel l'amant est secrètement introduit (par sa soeur religieuse!) le jour où s'y rend une 'brigata', une compagnie de femmes dont fait partie la veuve et, finalement, une rencontre chez la veuve même, qui habite le troisième étage d'un immeuble, tout échoue. L'immeuble en question est habité

---

85 Liste que le lecteur pourra continuer, les phantasmes érotiques étant ce que nous avons de moins personnel!

par des femmes seules, madonna Lionora au premier, au deuxième monna
Pasquina, et au quatrième monna Onesta. La pauvre veuve, quant elle reçoit son
amant, se trouve prise entre ses voisines du dessous et ses voisines du dessus.
Et l'amant, pour éviter la découverte doit se suspendre sous le balcon. Une fois
les voisines parties, l'amant remonte dans l'appartement, mais dit à Checca qu'il
pourra l'aimer, mais par terre. D'ailleurs elle est quand-même déshonorée et son
amant finit par l'abandonner; toutefois elle en trouvera d'autres. Donc ici la
narrativité argumentative est en quelque sorte suspendue: Ce n'est pas le résultat
(succès ou échec), mais la répétition, l'itérativité qui compte.

Deux observations à propos de cette nouvelle: La narrativité est faible, comme
nous l'avons déjà constaté: l'amant a quand-même accompli un acte qui dans
d'autres versions du même motif est qualifié d'héroïque (il essaie de sauver la
réputation de sa bien-aimée au péril de sa vie)[86] Cet acte aurait donc pu être une
affirmation de l'amour au niveau de l'argumentation narrative. La dame et
l'amour auraient été valorisés par la conduite héroïque de l'amant. Mais chez
Sercambi, il n'en est rien; tout au contraire l'amant en tire la conclusion bien
prudente qu'il ne faut pas trop se risquer. La femme est déshonorée, mais la
nouvelle ne se termine pas non plus sur ce coup narratif, mais sur le topos sur la
femme qui, libidineuse, saura toujours réaliser son désir. Et comme pour la
nouvelle précédente, pas d'offre d'identification avec un des personnages, à
moins que ce ne fût le gentilhomme. Seulement, dans cette alternative, le lecteur
s'identifiera alors avec sa prudence et non pas avec son amour. L'identification
comportera donc une certaine distance.

L'autre remarque concerne l'autorité. Dans la nouvelle analysée précédem-
ment, l'opinion publique joue déjà un rôle important, mais la famille y tient un
rôle aussi. Ici, l'autorité punitive n'est constituée, ni par le père, ni par les
frères, ni par le mari (Checca est veuve), mais par d'autres femmes seules,
femmes qui, dit Sercambi, envient à Checca sa bonne fortune.

Ouvrons une petite parenthèse: dans les nouvelles du domaine courtois il
aurait été tout indiqué de neutraliser cette autorité en disqualifiant "le punisseur
virtuel", p. ex. en faisant découvrir que les femmes jalouses seraient coupables
de la même immoralité dont elles accusent Checca.[87] Chose plus curieuse: les
voisines admettent leur envie: elles n'ont pas profité de l'occasion, donc elles ne
veulent plus de la compagnie de Checcha.[88]

---

[86] Cf. lord Grenville dans *La Femme de trente ans* de Balzac (éd. P.-G. Castex.) éd. de la
Pléïade vol. II, Paris 1976, p. 1102.

[87] Cf *Décaméron* I,4; III,1; IX,2.

[88] Elles répondent: "Di tale erba o fieno ne fusse pasciuta la nostra ronzina" p. 99[5-6]. La

Dans les deux nouvelles, la femme est couverte de mépris, mais sans qu'un autre protagoniste résulte sensiblement mieux traité. La réalité semble citée pour être condamnée (et en ceci les deux nouvelles sont peut-être réalistes). Mais ouvrons une petite parenthèse sur un autre genre:

Je peux à ce propos renvoyer à mon analyse faite ici même il y a quelques années, du Miracle 26 des *Miracles de Nostre Dame par personnages*.[89] Dans ce miracle, une femme mariée tue son beau-fils parce que l'on dit qu'elle a une relation amoureuse avec lui (dans la source de ce miracle,[90] cette rumeur est qualifiée de fausse) La peur de la voix publique est telle qu'une pauvre femme tue celui par qui le scandale arrive, même si c'est un innocent.[91]

A lire Sercambi, on s'aperçoit de quelques aspects de la vie quotidienne qui n'existent guère que comme présupposés dans la tradition courtoise, et dans les autres recueils de nouvelles populaires. Les personnages de Sercambi, souvent condamnés d'avance par l'auteur, plient sous le fardeau d'une réalité qu'ils doivent accepter, qu'il le veuillent ou non. Leurs utopies sont d'une modestie parfois déprimante ou bien reléguées dans le domaine de la religion, ou dans l'ailleurs des quelques contes de fées.[92]

Chez Sercambi l'on trouve, non pas le sourire désabusé qui caractérise d'autres nouvelles populaires (les choses sont ce qu'elles sont), mais un dégoût fasciné. Son moralisme, voire probablement son radicalisme religieux, le porte à condamner l'oeuvre de la chair qu'il tolère tout juste dans le mariage, conçu comme une barrière contre le torrent du désir, sur la force de résistance de

---

métaphore est évidemment sexuelle.

[89] Gustave Lanson: & Robert, Ulysse (éd) *Miracles de Nostre Dame par personnages, d'après le manuscrit de la bibliothèque nationale*. Société des Anciens Textes Français, Paris 1876-1883 ainsi que mon analyse "Miracles...".

[90] Gautier de Coincy: *Les Miracles de Nostre Dame* I-IV. éd. Frédéric Koenig, *Textes littéraires français* 176, Genève 1955-70.

[91] Si la première littérature courtoise est exaltante: offre de fortes possibilités d'identification avec des personnages positifs et héroïque, un trait important relie pourtant cette littérature courtoise aux formes populaires de la nouvelle; dans les deux genres, les rumeurs, le qu'en dit-on, la renommée jouent un rôle prépondérant: un chevalier doit relever un défi ou défendre la renommée d'une dame. Dans les nouvelles populaires, on assiste, dans un milieu beaucoup plus terne et terre à terre aux conséquences qui frappent ceux qui transgressent les tabous sociaux. C'est vues sur l'arrière-fond de ces phénomènes que les ruses et réalisations érotiques (si souvent camouflées) prennent toute leur si gnification: dans un monde livré au paraître, les valeurs doivent rester bien souvent secrètes.

[92] Il existe dans la nouvelle populaire d'autres utopies: l'action collective (Nicolas de Troyes: *Le Grand Parangon...*, nouvelle *40*) ou le cri de révolte. Cf. Sacchetti: nouvelles *201* et *202*.

laquelle Sercambi ne se fait pourtant guère d'illusions. Évidemment, ce n'est pas dans le couple que Sercambi irait chercher ses valeurs utopiques.

Et pourtant la vie quotidienne est là avec tous les problèmes qu'elle pose. L'amour est là, et l'on a vite fait de s'apercevoir qu'il ne se réduit pas au désir effréné (et monotone), pour lequel Sercambi emploie souvent les termes physiologiques les plus vulgaires. Dans les deux nouvelles sur lesquelles je me suis un peu attardé, ainsi que dans quelques autres, seulement évoquées en passant (ou passées sous silence) l'enjeu est tout aussi grave que dans nombre de nouvelles de Boccace: deux femmes cherchent – désespérément, dirait-on, si l'on devait en juger d'après les pseudo-faits présentés – à se faire une vie, à réaliser des rapports amoureux; deux femmes d'un certain âge qui ne trouvaient aucune justification de leur désir dans le système idéologique officiel (l'une est trop vieille pour avoir des enfants, l'autre est veuve). Et Sercambi n'est pas fait pour comprendre leurs problèmes. Seule sa fascination lui fait tout enregistrer. A nous de déchiffrer de tels messages avec d'autres clefs.[93]

Les problèmes du couple s'imposent dans toutes les cultures, mais les cultures s'imposent souvent aux problèmes et à leurs solutions possibles. Nous distinguons clairement, dans les *Novelle* et particulièrement dans nos deux exemples, aussi bien le rôle modélisant de la culture que les limites des modélisations culturelles. La littérature, importante modélisation culturelle, peut condamner certains comportements. Elle peut aussi les passer sous silence. Sercambi, tout en les condamnant, donne des comportements à voir qui sont rarement thématisés. Ces tentatives de réalisation suivies d'échec ont dû constituer l'état normal de bien de civilisations;[94] elles forment l'arrière-fond grisâtre sur lequel se détachent les merveilleuses aventures inventées dans quelques chefs- d'oeuvres (et répétées chez bien des épigones).

---

[93] Seul un Bandello enregistre certains 'faits-divers', une prostituée ou une servante d'un prêtre qui se tuent par désespoir, mais ces couples malheureux n'ont pas droit à un développement stylistique en registre tragique et provoquent souvent l'étonnement plus que la pitié.cf. *Transformations* ... p. 188. Il s'agit des nouvelles I, 50; ii,39; III, 31 et 58.

[94] A bien réfléchir, Sercambi ne décrit pas une société tout à fait immobile, mais une civilisation communale qui offre quand-même certains échappatoires. A poursuivre nos deux nouvelles, on pourrait s'imaginer que finalement nos deux braves femmes trouvent le bonheur; seulement, ce bonheur ne serait certainement pas enregistrable dans les codes culturels contemporains.

Gender and genre: short and long forms in the saga literature

By: JOSEPH HARRIS, *Harvard University*

> *Ma ð r er manns gaman.*
> *Hávamál*

The male world of the *þættir* (singular: *þáttr*) or short stories of the Old Norse-Icelandic saga literature can be exemplified in a telling form by the thirteenth- or fourteenth-century tale about Gestr of the Norns, *Norna-Gests þáttr*.[1] The guest, a vistor from the distant pagan and heroic past, finds his way to the court of the first Christian king of Norway, Óláfr Tryggvason (the year would have been 998). An atmosphere of tension accompanies the stranger, who is not Christian but has been primesigned; and the mystery peaks when Gestr, challenged by a wager, produces a fragment of a golden saddle buckle that had belonged to the ancient hero Sigurðr Fáfnisbani. Pressed for an explanation, the old man begins his reminiscences of the heroic age with the story of Sigurd's youth, including a minor incident in which Gestr, then Sigurd's servant, acquired the buckle, and goes on to the story of Sigurd's death at the hands of his brothers-in-law. The next day Gestr's saga-telling continues with an account of Brynhildr's death and Gestr's experience with the sons of Rag-

---

[1] Critical text in Ernst Wilken, ed., *Die prosaische Edda im Auszuge nebst Vǫlsunga-saga und Nornagests-tháttr*, Theil I: Text (Paderborn, 1877), pp. 235-261. (Wilken's 2nd ed. rev. of 1912 omits the introductory discussions; cf. there pp. vi-vii.) There are two versions: *Flateyjarbok: En samling af norske konge-sagaer mid indskudte mindre fortællinger*, [ed. C. R. Unger and G. Vigfússon] 3 vols. (Christiania, 1860-68), I, 346-359; and *Norrøne skrifter af sagnhistorisk indhold*, ed. Sophus Bugge, I [=Det norske oldskriftselskabs samlinger, VI] (Christiania, 1864), 47-80 [from "S" (= MS. AM 62) with readings from *Flateyjarbók*]. See further Nora Kershaw (Chadwick), ed. and tr., *Stories and Ballads of the Far Past* (Cambridge, 1921), pp. 11-12 (pp. 14-37 translate "A", a text close to Wilken and *Flateyjarbók*); Friedrich H. von der Hagen, *Volsunga- und Ragnars-Saga nebst der Geschichte von Nornagest*, Altdeutsche und altnordische Helden-Sagen, vol. 3, 2nd ed. rev. Anton Edzardi (Stuttgart, 1880), pp. lxii-lxix (pp. 345-397 translate Bugge's edition of S). The literature on the story is cited in Joseph Harris and Thomas D. Hill, "Gestr's 'Prime Sign': Source and Signification in Norna-Gests þ áttr," *Arkiv för nordisk filologi* 104 (1989), 103-122.

narr Loðbrók. The reminiscences conclude with the virtues of a series of six kings ranging from the fifth to the ninth centuries, all from Gestr's direct experience. Now Gestr volunteers the explanation of his destiny: when he was an infant, spae-wives (*nornir*) came to his home; the first two prophesied good, but the third said he should live no longer than the candle beside him would burn. He now carries the candle with him. Having lived three hundred years, he had come to Olaf to be baptized; and after a short period as one of the king's retainers, he quietly lighted his candle and expired in Olaf's presence.

Here Olaf's all-male court frames narratives from the pre-Christian past; the retainers and, especially, the king himself evaluate Gestr and his old stories against an implicitly masculine, Christian, and courtly standard, and the consummation of Gestr's life is acceptance into the retinue, baptism, and death in the very presence of the king as his candle burns out. The only "couple" here is obviously the lord and his loving warrior, but the story is not totally without women, for most of Gestr's old lore paraphrases Vǫlsung and Nibelung material which, of course, prominently concerns women – Sigrdrífa/Brynhildr, Guðrún, Grímhildr, Oddrún, Svanhildr – and could be described as a series of misalliances. Gestr's mysterious harping included a lay, "the ancient Wiles of Guðrún," but the centerpiece of his saga-telling was his account of Brynhild after Sigurd's murder, including a text of "Brynhild's Hell-ride" that deviates interestingly from that of Codex Regius of the Elder Edda. As Gestr concluded his account of Brynhild's pagan funeral, her flyting with a troll-woman, and this ogress's final shriek and leap from a cliff, the audience of retainers shouted "That's fine! Go on and tell us some more!"[2] But the king, mindful of their spiritual welfare, intervened: "You need not tell us any more about things of that kind," and continued: "Were you ever with the sons of Lothbrok?"[3] The only other women in *Norna-Gests þáttr* are the norns, the prophetic, semi-divine vagabonds, who determined Gestr's fate ages ago, and Gestr's own mother who, like Meleager's, preserved her son's life-token, the candle.

In literature a long life, especially a supernaturally long life – we find the device from the early Old English *Widsith* to the Čapek-Janaček *Makropoulos Case* – is an opportunity to display a slice of history or history *tout court*,[4] and *Norna-Gests þáttr* presents its audience with a version of history in which

---

2   Translations from Kershaw (Chadwick), here p. 33.

3   Kershaw (Chadwick), pp. 33-34.

4   For *Norna-Gests þáttr* in this connection see Friedrich Panzer, "Zur Erzählung von Nornagest," in *Vom Werden des deutschen Geistes: Festgabe Gustav Ehrismann...*, ed. Paul Merker and Wolfgang Stammler (Berlin and Leipzig, 1925), pp. 27-34, and Margaret Schlauch, "*Widsith, Víthförull,* and Some Other Analogues," *PMLA* 46 (1931), 969-987.

different eras are corollated with different conceptions of "the couple." The most ancient pre-Christian stage begins with a family, but Gestr's father presides over a household which is the scene of a rite performed entirely by women; the religious atmosphere is primitive, pre-heroic, inhabited by nameless collective female powers to which the individual male is subject. The second stage features heroic individuals of both sexes, together with the tragic couples and triangles of the Vǫlsung-Nibelung stories; woman does not control fate, but in the person of Brynhild she participates fully in the heroic struggle against it. The gods are individual and male, disposal of the dead is by fire; in short, it is the pre-Christian heroic age. Olaf, however, puts an end to tales of cremation and proud, violent suicides and adultresses like Brynhild and pointedly turns the saga-telling to an all-male, military milieu verging on the Christian period: "Were you ever with the *sons* of Lothbrok?" And the remainder of Gestr's account of "history as I witnessed it" is a survey of kings and courts ending with the most Christian, Louis the Pious. The final stage, the framing setting in Olaf's court, implicitly stretches on to the writer's present.

Norna-Gests þáttr is not isolated in the saga literature; its analogues include a group of brief anecdotes in which Óðinn or some other representative of the pagan past entertains a Christian king and his men,[5] but it has a close twin in the *Tale of Tóki Tókason*.[6] Tóki was fated to live through two life-times and sought out St. Olaf to complete his primesigning with baptism, "and he wore his white baptismal clothing until his dying day." Tóki's saga-telling mentions no women and reflects only military *Männerbünde* comparable to Norna-Gestr's service with the sons of Lothbrok; though the setting is pre-Christian, the purpose in *Tóka þáttr* is less a contrast with the Christian present than a comparison of Hrólfr kraki, the great Danish hero-king, and his warriors, with the similar figure from Norway, Hálfr, and his comitatus, the Hálfsrekkar.

Further, we may be justified in seeing in a third story, *Þorsteins þáttr skelks*,[7] a less obvious analogue of this group of tales: The Icelander Þor-

---

5   Discussed in Harris and Hill; an analogue omitted there is to be found in *Flateyjarbók*, II, 397-398: before vanishing into the sea Þórr tells tales of the past which include his slaying demonic women.

6   *Tóka þáttr Tókasonar* is found in *Flateyjarbók*, II, 135-138 and in *Fornar smásögur úr Noregs konunga sögum*, ed. Edwin Gardiner, with a foreword by Sir William A. Craigie (Reykjavík, 1949). Translations mine.

7   Found in *Flateyjarbók* and *Fornar smásögur*; the literature on the story is cited in John Lindow, "*Þorsteins þáttr skelks* and the Verisimilitude of Supernatural Experience in Saga Literature," in *Structure and Meaning in Old Norse Literature: New Approaches to*

steinn is among Olaf Tryggvason's retinue on a progress; in the middle of a spooky winter night Þorsteinn went alone to the privy, an outhouse fitted with two rows of eleven seats. A devil popped up out of the innermost seat, identifying himself as a figure from the heroic age, Þorkell hinn þ unni (Thorkel the Thin) who fell in the battle of Brávellir with King Haraldr Wartooth. Þorsteinn began asking him about the torments of Hell: no hero bears them better than Sigurd Fáfnisbani and none worse than Starkaðr the Old, who screams in pain. Now Þorsteinn begs the fiend to "Howl like Starkad, just for a little,"[8] and an escalating series of three mighty howls follows as the goblin moves several seats nearer with each howl. The last scream knocked Þorsteinn into a coma, but just then King Olaf had the church bell rung, and the devil fled groaning back down the privy. Þorsteinn had, of course, been playing for time and banking on the screeches waking King Olaf, who would know what to do. The folktale motif of the boy who does not know what fear is emerges in a concluding dialogue with the king in which Þorsteinn receives the new nickname of *skelkr* "shudder." Basically, however, this þ áttr is a polished Christian satire on the old pagan heroes, conceived with real humor and realized in snappy dialogue that I have not tried to paraphrase. But the story is also, arguably, a parody of the type of story represented by *Norna-Gests þáttr* and *Tóka þáttr*. Here the wanderer through time is not primesigned but a pagan hero; he does not enter the hall to stand before the king on his high seat but sidles up to a retainer on the toilet seat; his encounter with the Christian does not end with baptism, acceptance by the Männerbund, and death near the king, but with the plunge back into the privy (a kind of baptism!), rejection, and eternal life in suffering. In the architecture of the privy, travestying that of a noble hall, and in the devil's moving from seat to seat we might see parody of a motif like that of *Tóka þáttr* where the hero goes along the benches trying the strength of each retainer in order to find his level and his seat; the comparison of ancient heroes – a historical *mannjafnaðr* or comparison of men – reminds again of *Tóka þáttr*, while the vilification of Starkaðr in comparison with Sigurd is reminiscent of *Norna-Gests þáttr*. In any case, whether or not the parodistic reading is justified, it is certain that women are completely absent and the value structure of the story is based entirely on king, court, and muscular Christianity.

Textual Analysis and Literary Criticism, ed. John Lindow, Lars Lönnroth, and Gerd Wolfgang Weber (Odense, 1986), pp. 264-280.

8   Translation by Jacqueline Simpson, *The Northmen Talk: A Choice of Tales from Iceland* (London and Madison, 1965), pp. 152-155, here p. 154.

A cruder analogue, but a richer subject for gender analysis, is called *Sǫrla þáttr*.[9] We can recognize, as in *Norna-Gests þáttr,* three or four narrative segments that represent stages of history. The first is a mythic prelude in which the actors are the old gods, here distorted in another Christian satire, but this time a humorless one. Freyja is Odin's mistress; one day she sees where four dwarves are forging a magnificent necklace (elsewhere called the Brísingamen); they refuse to sell it but agree to give it to her in return for four nights of sex. Odin heard how Freyja had acquired the jewelry and determined to punish her by sending Loki to steal it; Loki managed this by turning into a fly, then a flea. Freyja begged Odin to return the necklace and he relented on condition that Freyja agree to cause a quarrel between certain kings who would live in the distant future; the fight was to be eternal unless "there be some Christian man so brave and so much favoured by the great good fortune of his liege lord that he shall dare to take arms and enter among the combatants and slay them."[10] Odin's conditions, of course, predict the course of the rest of the story, a narrative trajectory ultimately modeled on salvation history. In this first, mythic stage of history, then, "the couple" is illegitimate, and woman is presented in her lowest form as bitch-goddess; foreknowledge and design of the future stem from the weak and immoral Odin but are carried out by the evil goddess. As in *Norna-Gests þáttr*, fate is female and can be broken only by a Christian man, a member of the king's Männerbund.

The second narrative stage is the pre-Christian heroic age which culminates in a version of the *Hjaðninga víg*, the widely-known story of Heðinn's elopement with Hildr, daughter of Hǫgni. Prefixed to this is the short but complicated *fornaldarsaga* of Sǫrli, a Norwegian viking, who slew King Hálfdan of Denmark to acquire his precious warship; later Sǫrli, accompanied by his own father, encountered the sons of Hálfdan, Hákon and Hǫgni, in battle. The only survivors of the two families were Sǫrli and Hǫgni; having orphaned each other, they became blood brothers, "and both remained true to their oaths as long as they lived."[11] When Sǫrli finally fell in one of his viking raids, Hǫgni avenged him. Sǫrli's story has a chaste all-male cast; the precious object is not acquired by

---

9   *Flateyjarbók*; *Fornar smásögur*; and editions of the *fornaldarsögur*.

10   Translation by Kershaw (Chadwick). On connections between *Sǫrla þáttr* and *Þorsteins þáttr uxafóts* (*Flateyjarbók; Íslendinga þættir*, ed. Guðni Jónsson [Reykjavík, 1945]) see Alan L. Binns, "The Story of Þorsteinn Uxafót," *Saga-Book of the Viking Society* 14 (1953-55), 36-60, esp. 38-42: Þorsteinn is the son of Ívarr ljómi and in one episode ends a feud between "dead" pagans by administering a lasting death; like the episode of Ívarr's intervention, Þorsteinn's is put into a Christian perspective.

11   Kershaw (Chadwick), p. 48.

Freyja's unpleasant means, and good clean violence leads to that most masculine of fantasies, the *Waffenbruderschaft.* (More precisely, the fantasy is of a man's meeting his match in battle and, after fighting to a draw, creating a brother-hood of arms: this fantasy is found most famously, perhaps, in Gilgamesh's wrestling with Enkidu, but the violent inception of the friendship of Robin Hood and Little John also comes to mind.) The "couple" in this phase is not the king and his retainer but its more primitive prototype, the "warrior male" and his double – if I may borrow for a moment from the language of Klaus Theweleit in his *Männerphantasien.*[12] This stage of Hǫgni's life is free of women and woman-borne fate, but in the next phase of the story female elements re-enter.

Heðinn is a pirate-king of Serkland, imagined perhaps as the Barbary Coast. Alone in a forest he meets a goddess, whom we deduce to be Freyja though she calls herself by the valkyrie name Gǫndul. This scene and Heðinn's subsequent meetings with Gǫndul have a strongly erotic aspect, but her charms are used with a purpose, to infect Heðinn with the desire to surpass King Hǫgni. When he arrives in Denmark, Heðinn is made welcome, and the two heroes compete to a draw in all manner of sporting tests; finally they swear blood-brotherhood and promise to share everything equally. But Sǫrli's model cannot be recreated with women on the scene to spoil the warrior idyll; we now learn that Hǫgni has a wife and as only child a daughter whom he loves exceedingly. And now Heðinn again encounters Gǫndul who gives him a drink of forgetfulness and reawakens his sense of emulation: for his honor's sake, she persuades him, he must do away with Hǫgni's wife and abduct the daughter Hildr by force. The author explains: "The wickedness and forgetfulness contained in the ale which Hethin had drunk had so got the better of him that there seemed to him to be no alternative, and he had not the slightest recollection that he and Högni were 'foster-brothers.' "[13] Meanwhile Hildr has seen the future in dreams and tries to reason with Heðinn but realizes that "in this case you are not your own master." The murder of the queen in a sort of sacrifice may pattern with the acquisition of a valued object in the first two parts of the þáttr; afterward Heðinn again meets Gǫndul, again drinks, falling asleep in her lap; Gǫndul devotes them all to Odin, and Heðinn awakens to catch a glimpse of her disappearing, "big and black." He now understands the evil he has done, but the murder has barred any retreat; the abduction and pursuit must proceed as in the traditional versions of the story.

---

[12] *Male Fantasies,* tr. Stephen Conway, Erica Carter, and Chris Turner, 2 vols. (Minne-apolis, 1987-89; originally Verlag Roter Stern, 1977-78).

[13] Kershaw (Chadwick), pp. 51-52.

Heðinn finally makes a stand on the island Hoy; when the two men meet, both seem to understand the agency behind the murder and abduction, but they embrace their doom with tragic nobility. Because of Freyja's evil magic any man slain in the battle would have to start up and fight again and again, and the torture of this battle lasted, not until Ragnarǫk as in more traditional versions, but 143 years until the first year of King Olaf Tryggvason's reign in 995. Meanwhile Hildr, whose name means "battle" and who bears the blame for the *Hjaðninga víg* in more traditional versions – Hildr sat in a grove and watched. This third section of *Sǫrla þáttr*, then, is heroic in a full-blooded sense that makes it comparable to the Vǫlsung story in *Norna-Gests þáttr:* the setting is pre-Christian, men and women both have an opportunity to feel and to struggle gallantly. But the era is cursed and the "couple" is ill-fated; a wife and mother must be crushed beneath a viking ship, while an abducted bride must spend an immensely long wedding night watching her father and her husband, the would-be blood brothers, kill each other: male *Waffenbruder-schaft* is wrecked by devilish pagan interference, an interference gendered female. These fundamentally noble heathens never have a chance against the corrupting sex and magic of the goddess.

The fourth and last section of the þáttr takes place in the early days of the Christian present and is briefly told: Olaf and his warrior retinue land on Hoy, and Ívarr ljómi, a good Christian strengthened by the luck of his king, has the honor of giving the *coup de gracè* to Hǫgni, Heðinn, and all their good men. The theology of this conclusion is not learned, but death is presented as a release from torment, and the basic pattern of salvation history – divine in-tervention in the history of calamities that was the pagan world – is not hard to see. Interestingly enough no disposition of Hildr is mentioned; we are left with the image of her seated in a grove and watching the battle, and there she seems to belong. In the Christian present "the couple" is constituted by the king and his warrior Ívarr in the company of their comrades-at-arms.

The four stories mentioned so far show a common attitude toward history, religion, and gender, inclusion and exclusion, in short a common value structure. With this pattern established, let me pause briefly to place these short narratives in the context of the saga literature generally. The literary study of þættir might be said to begin with Wolfgang Lange's 1957 article "Einige Bemerkungen zur altnordischen Novelle."[14] Before Lange excellent historical and editorial work was done on individual stories, but glimpses of

---

[14] *Zeitschrift für deutsches Altertum* 88 (1957), 150-159.

the place of short narratives in what Northrop Frye called "an order of texts" are few and far between.[15] The importance of Lange's modest article is that it brought precisely this sense of a literary-historical order to bear and first mooted questions of genre that continue to be fruitful. I had not discovered Lange, however, when I began working on the þáttr in 1967; my inspiration came instead from T. M. Andersson's newly published *The Icelandic Family Saga: An Analytic Reading*.[16] Analysis of narrative structure gave me a key, I thought, to justifying some order among the hundreds of unordered short stories I had been reading in textual conglomerates such as *Morkinskinna* and *Flateyjarbók*; at the same time Andersson's method seemed to ignore or suppress all the fascinating problems of narratological theory and genre and so to be in need of supplementation. The subject of the short narrative forms blossomed from the end of the 1960's through the '80's, closely linked to the development of literary-theoretical interest in the saga literature generally.[17] Anyone who writes about short forms must have in mind some kind of contrast with long forms,[18] but beyond that general contrast any characterization of the þættir very quickly becomes characterization of one group of their texts. The same could be said of "saga" – how many brief references to "the saga" or "sagas" really refer only or principally to the family sagas? Despite theoretical gaps, however, the short narrative forms are now established as a particular set of themes within discourse on the saga literature. In evidence I would cite the most recent comprehensive history of Old Norse-Icelandic literature; Jónas Kristjánsson's *Eddas and Sagas: Iceland's Medieval Literature* from 1988 is a conservative work but the first to offer a separate chapter on þættir on the same level of organization as that of major genres such as the sagas of the Icelanders.[19] That is canonization!

The boundaries of the field, however, remain extremely vague. Most of the hundreds of short narratives in Old Norse-Icelandic are included within larger collections with a narrative arrangement; *Norna-Gests þáttr*, for example, i s

---

15 Discussed or registered in Joseph Harris, "Genre and Narrative Structure in Some *Íslendinga þættir*," *Scandinavian Studies* 44 (1972), 1-27, and in "Þ ættir," in *Dictionary of the Middle Ages*, ed. J. R. Strayer, vol. 12 (New York, 1989), pp. 1-6.

16 (Cambridge, Mass, 1967); the first result was a dissertation, "The King and the Icelander: A Study in the Short Narrative Forms of Old Icelandic Prose," Harvard 1969.

17 Bibliographical survey in Harris, "Þ ættir."

18 For interesting thoughts along these lines, see Mary Louise Pratt, "The Short Story: The Long and the Short of It," *Poetics* 10 (1981), 175-194.

19 Tr. Peter Foote (Reykjavík).

preserved as an episode in the longest of the biographies of Olaf Tryggvason (*Óláfs saga Tryggvasonar in mesta*). How can we tell what was an independent literary work, and wouldn't the very notion of independence – so central to our conception of literature – be a historically relative one?[20] Lange estimated the total corpus of þættir at over one hundred, but this guess shows more courage than clarity of generic conception. The "ethnic" or native terminology does not offer a safe guide,[21] but some regions of the hazy terrain of the short narrative have been convincingly mapped. In my last taxonomical effort of this kind I recognized seven fairly well-defined groups of þættir that account for at least sixty stories.[22]

The kind of cultural-historical question raised by the present conference has scarcely been posed of this corpus of tales. There have been literary interpretations of individual þættir, of course, and I did discuss what Wellek and Warren called "inner form" in the best-known subgroup, thirty-one texts that chart the changing relationship of an Icelander with a Norwegian king: twenty-six seemed to have certain common denominators of "theme," seventeen having "humanistic" and nine "religious" themes; and by a still more general measure, that of Weltanschauung, these short forms seemed to embody a high-medieval "comic" ethos by comparison to the heroic and tragic ethos of the longer sagas.[23] Very recently Vésteinn Ólason has interrogated a small subset of þættir for "the self-image of the free man"; he finds that the "essence of these tales seems to be a solution to the contradiction that a 'free' man increases his honour and his worth by subordinating himself to another man, the king."[24] This analysis is fully convincing, but to the extent that Vésteinn Ólason has rightly captured the "essence" of the þættir, their promise as a mirror of "the making of the couple" seems slight. Here the saga literature once again seems to stand distinctly outside the mainstream of European literature, to be in respect to the "couple" quite unlike *fabliaux, Mären, novelle,* or *Schwänke.* This conclusion runs counter to the Europeanizing trend in saga

---

20 The problem is discussed but not solved in Joseph Harris, "Theme and Genre in Some *Íslendinga þættir*," *Scandinavian Studies* 48 (1976), 1-28, and in "Þættir."

21 Ethnic and analytic genre terms were especially debated in three articles on "Genre in the Saga Literature" by T. M. Andersson, Lars Lönnroth, and Joseph Harris in *Scandinavian Studies* 47 (1975).

22 "Þættir."

23 "Theme and Genre."

24 "Den frie mannens selvforståelse i islandske sagaer og dikt," in *Medeltidens födelse*, Symposier på Krapperups Borg, 1, ed. Anders Andrén (Nyhamnsläge), 1989), pp. 277-286, here p. 285.

studies[25] and to the tendency of good essays by Walther Heinrich Vogt and Wolfgang Mohr on the "Wandel des Menschenbildes" from tragic to comic, as attested, in part, by such stories as our þættir.[26] It even runs counter to my own just paraphrased generalizations on the medieval, rather than heroic ethos of þættir! But the contradiction is more apparent than real. – Let us return to the stories in search of "the couple" or its absence.

One recognizable generic nucleus[27] comprises tales that focus on the clash of pagan and Christian cultures in the conversion period. In some of the group this generic idea is realized in a precise and personal form: one of the evangelizing kings is brought into contact with heathens; after a conflict, the pagans are converted and integrated into Christian society[28] – unless the conversion element is negated and, like Rauðr inn rammi, the resistant pagan is martyred.[29] One instance of the standard pattern would be *Þáttr Eindriða ilbreiðs* where a Noble Heathen undergoes testing in sports in direct competition with the king; the result is not quite brotherhood, as in the comparable struggle of Heðinn and Hǫgni, for Olaf's superiority is divinely sponsored.[30] But the young man is baptized and received into the retinue: "and the king took him into his own company with the greatest affection. And Eindriði never parted with the king again as long as they both lived, and he was always thought the most splendid of men." The young hero is unmarried and never brought into contact with a woman, though he does honor the pleas of his mother and sister in the archery contest – a version of the international Wil-

---

25 The trend is defined and reviewed by Carol J. Clover, "Icelandic Family Sagas (*Íslendingasögur*)," in *Old Norse-Icelandic Literature: A Critical Guide*, ed. Carol J. Clover and John Lindow, Islandica 45 (Ithaca, N. Y., 1985), esp. p. 251.

26 Vogt, "Wandel im altnordischen Menschentum," *Preussisches Jahrbuch*, Sept. 1923, pp. 315-322; Mohr, "Wandel des Menschenbildes in der mittelalterlichen Dichtung," *Wirkendes Wort*, 1. Sonderheft (1952), pp. 37-48; rpt. *Wirkendes Wort: Sammelband II* (Düsseldorf, 1963).

27 Some discussion of the idea of genre implied in this phrase is to be found in "Genre and Narrative Structure," pp. 22-23.

28 This group of þættir is further discussed in Joseph Harris, "Folktale and Thattr: The Case of *Rognvald and Raud*," in *Folklore and Medieval Studies*, ed. Carl Lindahl and Erika Brady (= *Folklore Forum* 13 [1980], 158-198), and in "Saga as Historical Novel," in *Structure and Meaning in Old Norse Literature*, pp. 187-219.

29 *Flateyjarbók* and *Fornar smásögur*.

30 *Flateyjarbók* and *Fornar smásögur*.

liam Tell motif. Continental influence is patent in this tale,[31] but just as obviously the basic value system we have already explored is at play here: what counts is male, Christian, and courtly; the highest good is to live and die with your king. The conversion group comprises at least twelve þættir; but not all stress the courtly Männerbund quite as much as our example. In one a mother urges compassion;[32] in another the only female character, a wife and mother, is instrumental in bringing the heathen father and son to God and to the king, and thus also in ending their estrangement from each other.[33] But in another story from this group, *Sveins þáttr ok Finns*, a divided family, apparently made up only of men, is restored to unity through conversion, but this time *without* female agency – clearly a story with the same value system we have been encountering.[34] The generational conflict that is often a concomitant of the conversion theme in the saga literature appears also in *Helga þáttr ok Úlfs*, which at least allows its single female a role in the family.[35] The three stories we have already examined, *Norna-Gests þáttr*, *Sǫrla þáttr*, and *Tóka þáttr*, are the best representatives of what in my taxonomy is a subgroup of conversion þættir in which the king is brought into contact with the heathen-heroic past; in a broader sense, however, any tale about conversion told from the vantage point of the securely Christian Middle Ages is an encounter between a doomed old order and a historically inevitable new order.

Finally, one tale from the conversion group constitutes an interesting exception to the absence of the "couple" as family; this is *Vǫlsa þáttr*, a spritely Christian satire with something of the air of Continental short-story forms.[36] It is

---

[31] Perhaps Irish influence is ultimately behind the "feat" in which the king juggles knives while running around his moving ship on the oars.

[32] *Svaða þáttr ok Arnórs kerlingarnefs* in *Flateyjarbók* and *Íslendinga þættir*.

[33] *Rǫgnvalds þáttr ok Rauðs* in *Flateyjarbók* and *Fornar smásögur*; for literature on the story see Harris, "Folktale and Thattr."

[34] In *Flateyjarbók* and *Fornar smásögur*; for literature see Elizabeth A. Rowe, "Searching for the Highest King: St. Christopher and *Þáttr Sveins ok Finns*," forthcoming in *Arkiv för nordisk filologi*.

[35] *Flateyjarbók* and *Fornar smásögur*; on generational conflict see Paul Schach, "Some Observations on the Generation-Gap Theme in the Icelandic Saga," *JEGP* 81 (1982), 196-203, and Harris, "Saga as Historical Novel."

[36] *Flateyjarbók* and *Fornar smásögur*; cf. Harris, "Historical Novel"; for significant recent work on the þ áttr see Gro Steinsland and Kari Vogt, "'Aukinn ertu Uolse ok vpp vm tekinn': En religionshistorisk analyse av *Vǫlsa þáttr* i *Flateyjarbók*," *Arkiv för nordisk filologi* 96 (1981), 87-106; they understandably omit mention of the misleading Herbert S. Joseph, "Völsa Þattr: A Literary Remnant of a Phallic Cult," *Folklore* 83 (1972), 245-252. The classic analysis is still Andreas Heusler, "Die Geschichte von Völsi, eine alt-

easy for a modern audience to appreciate because its skillful construction, satirical tone, and humorous sense of the absurd readily appeal to our skeptical tastes. The simplicity of the central narrative, told in short simple sentences, as well as the domestic setting and cast of characters, are reminiscent of fairytales; the unsaga-like characters are anonymous types – except for the comic touch of a named dog of unnamed masters. A long tradition lies behind the extant text, but in the form left by the final author the story assaults pagan superstition from a position of Christian rationalism with little overt moralizing. The message is principally embodied in the parody of paganism in which cult members worship an object called the *vǫlsi* – a pickled horse penis! This perversion of religion is related to the family's isolation and to the personal propensities of individual family members, and the Christian satirist implies a relationship between *social* inversion within the household dominated by the wife and this "unnatural" cult, instigated and perpetuated by the "proud" old woman. The party of the vǫlsi – the wife, the libidinous servant girl, and the rowdy son – are effectively contrasted with the anti-vǫlsi group: intelligent but passive father, virginally squeamish daughter, and plain, honest manservant, who would rather have a nice loaf of bread than the sacred fetish. The logic of Christian myth may lie behind the fact that the household's "fall" is blamed on the wife while the maiden daughter is first to note the "advent" of the saint King Olaf, who will convert the family to the True Faith; the author adds that "the old woman was slow taking to the Faith, but the farmer rather readier"; and "After they had been instructed in Whom they ought to believe and had come to recognize their Creator, they saw what a foul and unmanly way of life they had had and how deviant from all other good men." A "manly" standard within the family seems to depend on restoration of the traditional hierarchy as much as on religious orthodoxy.

The best-known group of þættir comprises thirty-one stories which concern, almost by definition, exclusively male relationships; their focus is principally on vertical relationships between the king and the Icelander (the relationships studied by Vésteinn Ólason under the aspect of "freedom"), but the stories also concern horizontal male relationships, mostly within the *Gefolgschaft*. Very few women or male-female couples play a role. At the end of his story Auðun does return to Iceland to care for his mother, but she is the only woman mentioned in this most celebrated of þættir.[37] The much admired and much trans-

---

nordische Bekehrungsanekdote," *Zeitschrift des Vereins für Volkskunde*, 1903, pp. 24-39 (rpt. in *Kleine Schriften*, II, 372-387). Translations mine.

[37] Íslenzk fornrit 6; among the more recent literature on the þáttr is Edward G. Fichtner, "Gift Exchange and Initiation in the *Auðunar þáttr vestfirzka*," *Scandinavian Studies* 51

lated *Story of Brandr the Generous* mentions no women at all,[38] and ten others of the group, including some of the best, have no use at all for women.[39] These thirty-one stories are based on a male dyad, a pair of roles usually filled by an Icelander and a king; the difference in power between the two roles is crucial, and the plots can be understood as variations on an alienation phase followed by a reconciliation phase.[40] This core plot structure is often framed by a journey from and return to Iceland, and a number of specific variations on the generic plot structure have been described. Essential in the present context, however, is that the only "couple" consistently in sight is male, and the generic plot normally ends in re-establishment of solidarity between them, though it is not strictly a solidarity of equals. There are some incidental women: Gísl Illugason is guarded in the king's jail by an old woman, probably only because the verse attributed to him in this situation addresses a woman.[41] Egill Síðu-Hallsson brought his wife and daughter to Norway, first leaving them in a rented house but later moving them right into the court, but the purpose of this brief episode is made clear when the king prophesies that the girl will be lucky: "and it turned out that way... for she is the mother of the holy bishop Jón."[42] This little passage may be an interpolation introduced as an oral variant ("Svá segir sumir menn..."); in any case it is a narrative excrescence. A protagonist's wife back in Iceland may be alluded to (*Þorgríms þáttr Hallasonar*),[43] or she may have a minor part to play in introductory events in Iceland before the journey to Norway (*Þórarins*

(1979), 249-272; but see especially the review of folk narrative connections in John Lindow, "Hreiðars þáttr heimska and AT 326: An Old Icelandic Novella and an International Folktale," *Arv* 34 (1978), 152-179, supplemented by Harris, "Folktale and Thattr."

38 *Brands þáttr ǫrva* in Íslenzk fornrit 4; recent literature: *Stories from the Sagas of the Kings*, ed. Anthony Faulkes (London, 1980), and Hermann Pálsson, "Brands þáttur örva," *Gripla* 7 (1990), 117-130; also cf. Sverrir Tómasson, "Vinveitt skemmtan og óvinveitt," in *Maukastella: færð Jónasi Kristjássyni fimmtugum* (Reykjavík 10. April, 1974), pp. 65-68 (mimeographed).

39 *Hreiðars þáttr heimska, Odds þáttr Ófeigssonar, Stúfs þáttr blinda, Þorsteins þáttr austfirðings, Þorsteins þáttr sǫgufróði, Þorvarðar þáttr krákunefs, Þáttr Þormóðar, Þorsteins þáttr skelks,* and *Þorsteins þáttr Síðu-Hallssonar.*

40 The structural analysis is elaborated in Harris, "Genre and Narrative Structure."

41 *Gísls þáttr Illugasonar* in Íslenzk fornrit 3; cf. Roberta Frank, "Why Skalds Address Women," in *Poetry in the Scandinavian Middle Ages*, ed. Teresa Pàroli (Spoleto, 1990), pp. 67-83.

42 *Egils þáttr Síðu-Hallssonar* in *Íslendinga þættir*, ed. Guðni Jónsson; translation mine.

43 Íslenzk fornrit 9.

þáttr Nefjólfssonar).[44] Since several of these stories relate the youthful adventures of a man who returns and settles in Iceland, we might expect to find the "couple" established at the end of the tale, but this is not the case. When it is told of an Icelander such as Hreiðarr heimski that "many men are descended from him," we must assume that mention of his marriage is simply elided.[45] Þorsteinn austfirðingr declines King Magnús's invitation to marry and settle in Norway; and though he settled in Iceland and was thought a *gæfumaðr* or man of good luck, the story does not say that he had descendants – probably because he is purely fictional.[46] Only *Ísleifs þáttr byskups*, which does deal with historical material, actually makes the establishment of a family part of the story's conclusion.[47]

In the dozen or so stories of this group in which a woman does play a more than nominal role, she is usually an agent (or merely an incident) in the alienation or reconciliation of the men. Bergljót, wife of Einarr Þambarskelfir, is prepared to intervene with arms against her husband to save Halldórr Snorrason,[48] and another great lady acts in a similar manner in *Steins þáttr Skaptasonar*.[49] There is nothing distinctively female about this role of helper and mediator, which is played much more often by men in the stories generally; there is, however, a passing interest in the dynamics of the royal or nearly royal couple in four or five stories. Take *Sturlu þáttr* for example: Sturla Þórðarson finds himself seriously on the outs with King Magnús Hákonarson; the intervention of a friend has not healed the breach, and now Sturla must spend some time in close quarters on shipboard with the King and Queen.[50] His

---

[44]   *Íslendinga þættir* (chapters 8-11 only; cf. Harris, "Genre and Narrative Structure," p. 3, n.).

[45]   So also for Auð unn vestfirzki of *Auðunar þáttr*.

[46]   Cf. Joseph Harris, "The King in Disguise: An International Popular Tale in Two Old Icelandic Adaptations," *Arkiv för nordisk filologi* 94 (1979), 37-81; Hermann Pálsson, "Early Icelandic Imaginative Literature," in *Medieval Narrative: A Symposium*, ed. Hans Bekker-Nielsen, et al. (Odense, 1979), pp. 20-30.

[47]   Ed. B. Kahle in *Kristni saga...* (Halle, 1905); the wooing and other incidents in the life of Ísleifr are treated as separate episodes in "Genre and Narrative Structure," p. 15; in retrospect I would treat them as episodes within the structural segment Conclusion.

[48]   *Halldórs þáttr Snorrasonar I* in *Íslenzk fornrit* 5; cf. Joseph Harris, "Christian Form and Christian Meaning in *Halldórs þáttr I*," *Harvard English Studies* 5 (1974), 249-264, and Faulkes, *Stories from the Sagas of the Kings*.

[49]   *Íslendinga þættir*.

[50]   Edited separately in Guð ni Jónsson, ed., *Sturlunga saga*, III (Íslendingasagnaútgáfan, 1954), 367-383; see discussion of manuscripts and semi-independent status of text, p. xi. Translations used here are from Simpson, *Northmen Talk*, but this is an incomplete ren-

reception among the crew and retainers is cool until he entertains them with a saga-recital; the queen sees the crowd and conceives an interest in hearing the story. The next day, in a passage famous for its implications about saga-entertainment or *sagnaskemmtun*,[51] the queen's mediation prevails to the extent of sending for Sturla to come to the poop-deck to entertain the royal couple. The saga-telling leads to permission to perform a praise poem before the king; and so, little by little and with much applause from the queen, Sturla is led into full favor and earns the king's accolade: "It's my opinion that you recite better than the Pope himself." Eventually Sturla achieves membership in the retinue and the title of *skutilsveinn*. Notice, incidentally, that the subject matter of Sturla's saga-telling is a *Huldar saga*, "about a huge she-troll"; here Christianity presumably plays no role, but the presentation of the demonized, primitive, female *Stoff* to an enthusiastic male audience is similar to the situation in *Norna-Gests þáttr*.[52]

In *Sturlu þáttr* and generally in these stories the female member of a couple shows more conciliatory good sense and goodwill than the male and is shown getting round him, getting her way by diplomacy or power or both. An amusing variation on the same idea occurs in the second of the þættir about Halldórr Snorrason where the generic apparatus of reconciliation comes to nothing, and the final interview of those old comrades Halldórr and King Haraldr parodically inverts a reconciliation scene: instead of appearing hat in hand before a king sitting in state in his beer hall, the Icelander breaks into the king's bedroom and stands towering, fully armed, over Haraldr and the queen as they lie in bed; and instead of presenting a gift or a poem or a task accomplished, Halldórr demands the queen's ring in payment for money owed him. Haraldr tries to temporize, but the queen intervenes: " 'Give him the ring,' said the queen. 'Can't you see the way he's standing over you, the killer?' "[53]

dering; see Julia McGrew and R. George Thomas, tr., *Sturlunga saga*, II (New York, 1974), pp. 489-499, for a complete translation. Úlfar Bragason, "Sturlunga saga: Atburðir og frásögn," *Skáldskaparmál: Tímarit um íslenskar bókmenntir fyrri alda*, 1 (Reykjavík, 1990), 73-88, demonstrates the influence of literary patterns on the supposedly raw historical *Stoff* of the *Sturlunga saga* complex partly in a detailed discussion of this story.

51 Cf. Hermann Pálsson, *Sagnaskemmtun Íslendinga* (Reykjavík, 1962), esp. pp. 52, 116, 168-169.

52 Huld may be the troll-witch of that name who took on the form of a mare to trample King Vanlandi to death in *Ynglinga saga*; however, the name is generic for "witch"; cf. Preben Meulengracht Sørensen, *Saga og samfund: En indføring i oldislandsk litteratur* (Copenhagen, 1977), pp. 162-163.

53 *Halldórs þáttr Snorrasonar II* in Íslenzk fornrit 5; translation from *Hrafnkel's Saga and*

In two stories, *Ǫgmundar þáttr dytts ok Gunnars helmings* and *Þorvalds þáttr tasalda*, an adventure among pagans is part of the story's generic reconciliation section and includes a conversion and marriage to a formerly heathen woman.[54] But the inclusion of a little conversion story as part of the reconciliation of king and Icelander is found most brilliantly realized in *Þórarins þáttr Nefjólfssonar*, where the retrospectively told conversion episode involves the mother of one of the protagonists. This generic juxtaposition resembles that found in the tale of the encounter of Þorsteinn skelkr with the devil, where the incident we examined in connection with narratives of the *Norna-Gests þáttr* type is set within an alienation-and-reconciliation framework concerning an Icelander and his king.

The well-made story of Hrafn Hrútfirðingr, also known by his mother's name as Guðrúnarson, probably gives more space to woman and family couples than any other of the group of thirty-one.[55] The long prelude in Iceland is a typical feud saga in little; Guðrún is the main figure (with a role a bit like that of the mother of Víga-Glúmr): she endures after the killing of her husband until her son will be old enough to take revenge, and she uses all her wiles to get him safely out of the country when he does. The second part in Norway is a quite regular alienation-reconciliation story, except for the prominence given women. Hrafn's offences begin with his attentions to his host's daughter, but she and her mother attempt to intercede for Hrafn. When the offences escalate and Hrafn is outlawed, the women drop out of the story, but when King Magnús Óláfsson is finally reconciled with Hrafn, the denouement includes marriage to the girl and fetching his mother from Iceland to join the newly established – mostly female – family in Norway. But this probably fictional tying-up of loose ends does not prevent the more genre-specific concluding formula: "Hrafn was ever after with King Magnús, as long as the king lived."

The wealthy widow Ása figures importantly in the story of a certain Þórðr, sans patronymic, who was satirically nicknamed for his association with her, Gull-Ásu-Þórðr, Rich-Ása's Thord.[56] The relationship, partly business, partly pleasure, is the cause of trouble, as the poor but energetic Icelander is seen in

---

Other Stories, tr. Hermann Pálsson (Harmondsworth, 1971); cf. Harris, "Genre and Narrative Structure," p. 19.

[54] A couple is encountered in the adventures in *Þórodds þáttr Snorrasonar* and in *Þorvalds þáttr;* Íslenzk fornrit 27: 255-261 (and pp. 1-li); Íslenzk fornrit 9: 119-126.

[55] Íslenzk fornrit 8, and W. H. Wolf-Rottkay, ed., *Altnordisch-isländisches Lesebuch* (Munich, 1967); translations mine.

[56] *Gull-Ásu-Þórðar þáttr* in Íslenzk fornrit 11; my translations.

Norway as a social climber. The main interest of the story, however, lies not in Ása and Þórðr as a couple, but in the clever way the underdog Icelander over-comes hostility and prejudice, and, like several others of the group, the story especially thematizes friendship. The relationships in question are among men, but the real point is an unsentimental conception of friendship as reciprocity for favors given. The story ends with marriage, social approval, and wealth.

A relationship to a woman is also the cause of trouble in a third story, *Óttars þáttr svarta*: the famous Icelandic poet had composed love verses about Olaf Haraldsson's queen. The reconciliation also comes, as so often, through poetry, but the queen too is active in the reconciliation.[57] The author of this anecdote – almost too brief to analyze – is interested in the ambiguous relationships within the royal couple and among the three characters. The situation is charged but inexplicit, perhaps not yet "triangular desire," but pointing in that direction.

Perhaps the funniest story of the group is one of the least unified, *Sneglu-Halla þáttr*.[58] Here Haraldr harðráði's rough and often bawdy sense of humor is on display from the very first episode, which involves clever repartee around the consummate male insult, passive sodomy. In the fuller and more original version, King Haraldr's queen, who did not like Halli, is mentioned near the beginning and reenters near the end of the þáttr where she criticizes the king for associating with the foul-mouthed poet; the incident goes like this:

[Halli was staring admiringly at a valuable silver-chased axe in the king's hand:] The king noticed that right away and asked whether the axe pleased Halli. He answered that he liked it very much. "Have you ever seen a better axe?" Halli answered, "I don't believe so." The king asked, "Would you let yourself be buggered for the axe?" "No," said Halli, "but it seems to me excusable that you would want to give the axe away the same way you acquired it." "And so it shall be, Halli," said the king, "you take it and make the best use of it: for it was freely given to me, and so I shall give it to you." Halli thanked the king. In the evening, when the company had sat down to their drinking, the queen told the king clearly that it was bizarre and not at all appropriate to give that treasure of an axe to Halli – "something which is hardly property for men of non-noble rank, bestowing

---

57   *Óttars þáttr svarta* is ch. 4 of "Sighvats þ áttr" in *Íslendinga þættir*; cf. the explanation in Harris, "Genre and Narrative Structure," p. 3 n., and Simpson's treatment in *Northmen Talk*.

58   *Íslenzk fornrit* 9; my translations.

it in return for his filthy language. Meanwhile, some men get little for their good service." The king answered that he himself would decide to whom he gave his treasures: "I do not want to turn Halli's words – those which are ambiguous – to the worse interpretation."[59]

King Haraldr goes on to offer the queen a further demonstration of linguistic ambiguity and how interpretation is a two-edged sword. He calls on Halli to compose an ambiguous verse about her – " 'and let's see how she takes it.' " The verse is racy and philologically difficult, but the gist is that she, Queen Þóra, is the person most suitable to perform certain sexual services for Haraldr. " 'Take him out and kill him,' said the queen, 'I will not put up with his slander.' The king commanded that no one be so bold as to lay a finger on Halli for this – 'but something can be done about it if you think some other woman is more suitable to lie beside me and be queen. And you don't know praise of yourself when you hear it.' " This is a triangular situation we know from modern life: the wife and the free-living friend as rivals for the established and powerful figure, the husband.

Another form of the triangle appears in the last of this group of stories I mean to mention, *Ívars þáttr Ingimundarsonar*.[60] Ívarr was at the court of King Eysteinn Magnússon and sent a message home to Iceland to a woman there, declaring his love and asking her not to marry anyone else. The messenger was Ívarr's own brother, but the brother betrayed Ívarr and married the woman himself. Ívarr had already arrived in Iceland when he learned of this situation, but he immediately returned to Norway and the king's court. Most of this very short story is occupied with King Eysteinn's attempts to discover the cause of Ívarr's resulting depression and then to cure it. The king's suggestions of the other-fish-in-the-sea cure and his offer of money are greeted glumly, but his third suggestion does work: "We'll talk about this woman to your heart's content for as long as you wish, and I'll devote my time to it. Sometimes a man's grief is soothed when he can talk about his sorrows." This idea has echoes not only in the *Roman de la Rose* but in the Norse *Hávamál*,[61] and

---

59 ÍF 9: 293-294; on the versions of the þáttr, cf. pp. cix-cxiv. The passage I have translated here is briefly discussed by Preben Meulengracht Sørensen, *The Unmanly Man: Concepts of Sexual Defamation in Early Northern Society*, tr. Joan Turville-Petre (Odense, 1983), p. 27, in the general context of defining *níð*, and compare Michael Minkov, "Sneglu Halli, 2: 11: *Dróttinserðr*," *Saga-Book of the Viking Society*, 22, pt. 5 (1988), pp. 285-286.

60 *Íslendinga þættir*; for manuscripts and editions see Ulset p. vii; translation from Hermann Pálsson, *Hrafnkels saga and Other Stories*.

61 *Roman de la Rose*, ll. 3099-3110; *Hávamál*, 121, 8-10; 124, 1-3; cf. Harris, "Theme and

the talking cure, as psychotherapy is sometimes called, must be universal. The original triangle situation obviously relates this story to a whole series of Icelandic sagas, *Bjarnar saga Hítdœlakappa, Kormaks saga, Gunnlaugs saga ormstungu, Hallfreðar saga vandrœðaskálds*, and *Laxdœla saga*, and beyond them to a worldwide narrative structure of triangular desire.[62] In all these sagas the couple that should have come into being but did not, the absent couple, haunts long texts that deal with the rivalry of two men. The desire they feel toward the same woman feeds on imitation, is the "imitative desire" of René Girard's triangle, and the jealousy between them is a bond to which we could assign different names. But what is interesting in the present context is the *contrast* with *Ívars þáttr*. In the full-length sagas the triangle is sustained to the death, and this is presumably what originally made the material *sǫguligt*, worth telling in a saga. But in the short story the spell of the triangle is broken, and the narrative retreats to the male dyad, the warrior and his loving lord. (In Germanic imaginative life, insofar as it is documented in literature, *this* "couple" is the older; one thinks, for example, of the OE Wanderer searching far and near for a lord who will not only cheer and support him but who would "know my loving thoughts" ["(minne) myne wisse"].) In the thirteenth-century saga literature the exploration of the erotic triangle belongs to Icelandic settings and to the longer genre, the sagas, but the þáttr-hero Ívarr returned to the court and the king. In terms of genre, one might say, exaggerating a bit, that Ívarr's story begins as a saga but reverts to þáttr status. In fact, the treatment is that of the short story throughout, and it is only through the comparanda that we know the initial situation was treated by preference in saga-length works. Within the story, however, the king replaces the woman and the rival; and while the triangular stories of the sagas end tragically, the þáttr takes leave of its hero, his cheerfulness restored, on what Northrop Frye might have called a comic note of incorporation or reincorporation into the courtly Männerbund. The closing benediction on Ívarr is "And he remained with King Eystein."

Our conclusions about the couple in þættir – at least about the couple in the sense of our conference theme – must be moderately negative. In the medieval North short narrative forms were *not* found notably suitable for exploring do-

---

Genre," p. 26, n. 29.

[62] The Baldr-Hǫðr-Nanna story as told by Saxo (book three) may be cut from the same cloth, and the tale of Helgi Hjǫrvarðsson, his brother Heðinn, and the valkyrie Sváva may have been more comparable in a more original form (*Helgakviða Hjǫrvarðzsonar*, prose after st. 30 to end).

mestic problems, but *Ívars þáttr* does point the way to anyone who would wish to pursue the problem of the couple in early Icelandic literature. The *skáldasǫgur*, the group of sagas chiefly about the lives of poets and constructed on an enduring love triangle, would be a beginning.[63] After that almost all the great family sagas would offer rich materials, and the student of the couple in these longer forms could build on the relatively rich secondary literature on aspects of gender already in place.[64] *Njáls saga* shows that the domestic couple could have a narrative significance even in the absence of a love triangle, but an irritant, a third factor, is necessary to the generation of a narrative, for the marriage portraits in the sagas contain few cries or whispers of post-Romantic inwardness. In the family sagas that irritant is usually competition, outward conflict, or some stage of a feud: for instance, the couple comes memorably to the fore in *Hávarðar saga Ísfirðings* in the context of delayed revenge. Two sagas would stand out, however, as especially important for the treatment of the couple: *Gísla saga Súrssonar* and *Laxdœla saga*. *Gísla saga* is the more intense and narrower of the two, showing the failure of most human institutions – oath brotherhood, servant-master loyalty, female same-sex friendship, blood kinship, kinship overvalued in incestuous desire, perhaps also religion – but it is the bond of the married couple that emerges from the story as the least weak.[65] A reading of *Laxdœla saga* from the point of view of the couple would have to be, I would argue, considerably more complicated. Admittedly the saga appears simple in the central constellation of Kjartan, Bolli, and Guðrún where it draws on the classic structures of triangular desire in the sense of René Girard.[66] The solution of the tension here is neither the institutionalization of the triangle as in the *skáldasǫgur* nor Ívarr's retreat to the male bond; instead *Laxdœla saga* revives the pattern of

---

[63] Cf. Bjarni Einarsson, *Skáldasögur: Um uppruna og eðli ástaskáldasagnanna fornu* (Reykjavík, 1961), and the contextualization by Clover, "Icelandic Family Sagas," esp. pp. 249-251.

[64] Especially conspicuous is Thomas Bredsdorff, *Kaos og kærlighed: En studie i islændingesagaens livsbillede* (Copenhagen, 1971); and cf. Clover's survey in "Icelandic Family Sagas," pp. 256-259.

[65] One of the most recent contributions to the study of gender-related themes in *Gísla saga* is Preben Meulengracht Sørensen, "Murder in Marital Bed: An Attempt at Understanding a Crucial Scene in *Gísla Saga*," in *Structure and Meaning in Old Norse Literature*, pp. 235-263.

[66] *Deceit, Desire, and the Novel: Self and Other in Literary Structure*, tr. Yvonne Freccero (Baltimore and London, 1966 [French original 1961]); cf. Eve Kosofsky Sedgwick, *Between Men: English Literature and Male Homosocial Desire* (New York, 1985).

the Vǫlsung-Nibelung story with two couples superseding but never quite dissolving the triangle and of course leading to a re-enactment of the tragic paradigm of the ancient heroic story. For its part *Gísla saga*, also famously haunted by the Vǫlsung material,[67] deploys its quadrangles and triangles in interlacements that are less predictable but no less tragic. But when we go beyond the core narrative to consider the sweep of *Laxdœla saga* from Unnr in djúpúðga through the unforgettable last words of Guðrún Ósvífsdóttir, it is clear that permutations of the triangle would not be adequate to the saga's discussion of sexual politics.

Our survey of þættir has delved into only two groups, totaling some forty-five short stories. Outside these groups a few texts may be more directly relevant to the thematics of the couple.[68] The jolly *Hróa þáttr heimska* comes to mind: there the socially modest Danish hero moves from the patronage of the king, Sven Forkbeard, to a wealthy marriage to the clever daughter of a famous Swedish lawman; the male world of the first part of the þáttr thus stands in contrast to Hrói's dependence on the wisdom of his wife (and her father) in the second part, and Hrói's trials eventuate in a good marriage, literally "the making of a couple." The author was, however, probably most interested in his nordicization of the central motifs of the story from the *senex cæcus* tale of the *Seven Sages*; moreover, *Hróa þáttr* is an isolated case.[69] My impression is that also *outside* the two main groups of þ ættir

---

67 See, for example, Heinrich Matthias Heinrichs, "Nibelungensage und Gísla saga," in *Beiträge zur deutschen und nordischen Literatur: Festgabe für Leopold Magon zum 70. Geburtstag, 3. April 1957*, ed. H. W. Seiffert, Veröffentlichungen des Instituts für deutsche Sprache und Literatur, 11 (Berlin, 1958), pp. 22-29, and Meulengracht Sørensen, "Marital Bed."

68 Conspicuously absent from our survey is the small group of þættir that deal with Icelandic feuds, texts such as *Gunnars þáttr Þiðrandabana* (Íslensk fornrit 11) and the first part of the *Hrafns þáttr* discussed above. These operate with the same narrative structure as the family sagas; in fact, the justly well-known *Þorsteins þáttr stangarhǫggs* served Andersson's *Family Saga* as a structural model for the feud saga, and the dearth of such feud þættir in the corpus has been thought due to their having been early absorbed into or expanded as feud sagas (Herbert S. Joseph, "The Þáttr and the Theory of Saga Origins," *Arkiv för nordisk filologi* 87 [1972], 95; cf. Clover, "Icelandic Family Sagas," pp. 291-294). Domestic relations probably come in for about the same amount of attention there as in the family sagas. *Gunnars þáttr*, for example, repeats an incident of *Laxdœla saga* in which Guðrún Ósvífsdóttir rides roughshod over her fourth husband at their wedding feast – an anecdote significant for cultural history but probably not part of a gender/genre pattern.

69 Dag Strömbäck, "En orientalisk saga i fornnordisk dräkt," in *Donum Grapeanum: Festskrift tillägnad överbibliotekarien Anders Grape på sextiofemårsdagen, den 7 mars 1945*

surveyed here, the short forms were not an important instrument for thinking through problems of the couple. Of the long forms, the saga genres, I have glanced only at the family sagas, but there, it seems to me, we do find a fairly extensive problematization of marriage, jealousy, and the politics of the couple. How can we explain this literary-historical pattern where long and short forms roughly reverse expectations formed from continental literature?

A hint may be given by the echoes of the mythic and heroic stories in the sagas, what has been called their heroic legacy, eddic perspective, or *eddischer Blick*.[70] Problematic love relationships in the Nordic mythic material, where they are common enough, tend to be seen from the male perspective;[71] but in the heroic poetry this problematics of the couple is registered to a great extent in women's voices or from a female point of view – so much so that a term like "heroine-ic poetry" would not be out of the question if it were not so unwieldy. It may be that the family sagas inherited not only the specific motifs and story-patterns noted by earlier scholars such as Guðbrandur Vigfússon and Magnus Olsen and not only their spirit and rhetorical structure as argued by the likes of W.P. Ker and T.M. Andersson, but also this aspect of their thematics.[72]

Against the eddic legacy of the family sagas we might set the *skaldic legacy* of the major groups of þ ættir. Of course our conventional term "skaldic poetry" covers a great variety of poetic phenomena over time and space, but one can recognize more or less central and more or less marginal areas, and praise of the ruler, especially in "court-meter" (*dróttkvætt*), is agreed to lie at the heart. Skaldic praise-poetry was, according to the stereotypes, presented by the poet before his lord in the presence of the warriors of the court; the dramatis

---

(Uppsala, 1945), pp. 408-444; rpt. in *Folklore och filologi*, Skrifter utg. av Gustav Adolfs Akademien för Folklivsforskningen 48 (Uppsala, 1970), 238-254.

[70] Andersson, "The Heroic Legacy," in *Family Saga*, ch. 3; Roberta Frank, "Onomastic Play in Kormakr's Verse: The Name Steingerðr," *Mediaeval Scandinavia* 3 (1970), 7-34, esp. 27-34; Ulrike Sprenger, *Praesens historicum und praeteritum in der altisländischen Saga* (Basel, 1951), esp. p. 17.

[71] Pointed out by Bjarni Einarsson, *Skáldasögur*, pp. 11-14, and Roberta Frank, "Onomastic Play," p. 27.

[72] See Andersson, *Family Saga*, for the earlier references; some later studies in this kind are: Anne Heinrichs, "Beziehungen zwischen Edda und Saga: Zur Interpretation zweier Szenen aus der Heiðarvíga saga," *Zeitschrift für deutsches Altertum und deutsche Literatur*, 99 (1970), 17-26; Oskar Bandle, "Isländersaga und Heldendichtung," in *Afmælisrit Jóns Helgasonar, 30. júní 1969*, ed. Jakob Benediktsson, et al. (Reykjavík, 1969), pp. 1-26; Haraldur Bessason, "Mythological Overlays," in *Sjötíu ritgerðir helgaðar Jakobi Benediktssyni 20. júlí 1977* (Reykjavík, 1977), I, pp. 273-292.

personae and scene are, therefore, also typical for the þættir we have surveyed, and a great many of the short stories are, like *Ívars þáttr* and *Sturlu þáttr*, stories of poets or saga-tellers. In an inventive article John Lindow suggested that the inherent ideology of such poetry correlated with its notoriously difficult, riddle-like style; it functioned as a kind of test or sign of initiation into the *drótt* or court: "Early skaldic poetry might, therefore, be regarded as a device for isolating non-members, i.e. the lower classes and women, from the *drótt*. It functioned, in effect, as a kind of secret language in which the members of the *drótt* could maintain their collective traditions in a special way and also communicate without being wholly understood by others, indeed to the exclusion of others."[73] Similarly the þáttr-hero wants to be included in his lord's favor and ranked among the retainers; it is, as we have seen, a value system based on the male dyad in the context of the Männerbund. Implicitly it excludes women, family, and the heterosexual couple.[74] Unlike the sagas, where the heroic legacy is woven into warp and woof, the þættir seem, as we have already seen, to fence off eddic influences with a distancing frame or to exclude them altogether; but the "skaldic legacy" is part and parcel of their stories.[75]

One is reminded of the comparison of the two verse forms by Haraldr harðráði, about whom so many þættir tell: he improvised a stanza in the easy eddic meter *fornyrðislag*, but immediately corrected himself: "That is badly composed, and I must make a second stanza and make it better."[76] The content of the better poem is quite similar, but the form is that of the elaborate court meter. (Presumably any women who happened to be marching along toward destiny at Stamford Bridge would have understood the first stanza but not the second! Obviously any theory can be pushed to absurdity.)[77] Like eddic verse the sagas were a relatively open form, expansive enough to accommodate several kinds of materials and influences and to develop several themes;

---

[73] "Riddles, Kennings, and the Complexity of Skaldic Poetry," *Scandinavian Studies* 47 (1975), 311-327, quotation: pp. 322-323.

[74] Sedgwick, *Between Men*, argues that even relationships that seem to exclude women are inscribed with the whole question of gender arrangements; p. 25 and passim.

[75] The chief instance of other eddic manifestations in þættir would perhaps be the incident in *Sneglu-Halla þáttr* in which Þjóðólfr Arnórsson is directed to compose verses portraying quarreling commoners, a smith and a tanner, first as Þórr and Geirrøðr, then as Sigurd and Fáfnir (Íslenzk fornrit 9: 267-269).

[76] So in *Heimskringla*; for the other sources, see Íslenzk fornrit 28: 187-188.

[77] On women skalds see Guðrún P. Helgadóttir, *Skáldkonur fyrri alda*, I (Akureyri, 1961).

open too in the sense of being self-explanatory and accessible to mixed audiences which would have shaped the treatment and thematic repertoire.

By comparison skaldic court verse and the central groups of þ ættir are closed forms, with a smaller range of themes and values implying, probably, a narrower audience. Consider again the example of Sturla Þ ó rðarson: he told a saga with what we might call "late eddic" content and featuring a demonized female; the audience ranged from the crew to the king, but especially appreciative was the queen. When Sturla recited a skaldic poem, however, it was explicitly for the king, though the queen listened in. Her approving comment was greeted by the king with irony: "Are you able to follow it quite clearly?" She extracts herself with a tactful ambiguity, but as a woman and a Dane she may have had two strikes against her as a critic of skaldic verse.[78] (Some comments in the sources suggest, though, that not every male ruler who was willing to pay for a poem could actually understand it.) Internally, then, we see two different audiences correlated with gender and genre, but who formed the audience of *Sturlu þáttr* itself, or of *Gísls þáttr* or *Stúfs þáttr* or any of them? There is no reason external to the texts to suppose the audiences actually restricted to any sort of Männerbund; yet in a vague way this narrower ancestry seems inscribed in the stories. Like courtly eulogy, stories of the kind we have been discussing had a limited future, but the structural limits of the genres or subgenres probably are an essential part of the high level of literary achievement we find among the þ ættir.

Our conference topic comprises two themes, the couple and short narrative forms, and invites the consideration of short forms as a favored instrument of medieval literature for consideration of the problems – copious in all ages – of the core of every family. For the continental mainstream this is undoubtably one of the roles of *fabliaux, Mären, novelle*, and the like, while the contemporary West Scandinavian literature of the thirteenth and fourteenth centuries seems to offer a contrast and counterinstance. The thesis of a favored nexus between short forms and the domestic theme of the couple should be viewed, however, as a special case of a more general hypothesis connecting gender and genre. At this deeper level the þ ættir constitute strong confirmatory evidence.

---

[78] Cf. Simpson, *Northmen Talk*, p. 4, n.

Zur Paarbeziehung in deutscher Märendichtung[1]
Sozialer Kontext und Bedingungen

Von WALTER BLANK, *Albert-Ludwigs-Universität, Freiburg*

In einer vor kurzem erschienenen Literaturgeschichte heißt es zur Einschätzung der deutschen Mären lapidar: Die "Mären stellen die eigentliche literarische Neuerung in der volkssprachlichen [deutschen] Literatur des 13. Jahrhunderts dar."[2] In der Tat gilt der Stricker (ab etwa 1220) als der Schöpfer dieser Gattung in Deutschland. Wenn es richtig ist, was Erich Köhler mit der Neuschöpfung literarischer Gattungen verknüpft, daß nämlich in einer neuen Gattung jeweils ein literarisches Gewand für Fragen gesucht wird, die im traditionellen Gattungskanon nicht adäquat unterzubringen waren,[3] dann bedeutet das in unserm

---

[1] Trotz der neueren Gattungsdiskussion des Märenbegriffs behalte ich diese Bezeichnung als Arbeitsbegriff für unsere Fragestellung hier bei. Denn selbst bei jenen Vertretern, die das Märe als eigene Gattung ablehnen (bes. J. Heinzle; H.-J. Ziegeler), besteht Übereinkunft darüber, daß mit dem von Hanns Fischer aufgestellten Märenkatalog von 219 kürzeren Erzähltexten (Studien zur deutschen Märendichtung, 2. Aufl. bes. v. J. Janota, Tübingen 1983) ein Erzähltypus im Kern erfaßt ist, der durch didaktische Funktion (J. Heinzle, Märenbegriff u. Novellentheorie. in: K.-H. Schirmer [Hg.], Das Märe. Darmstadt 1983, S. 91-110; ders., Geschichte der deutschen Literatur von d. Anfängen bis z. Beginn d. Neuzeit. Bd. II,2: Vom hohen zum späten Mittelalter. Königstein 1984, S. 174-180) und durch eine bestimmte Erzählform (H.-J. Ziegeler, Erzählen im Spätmittelalter. Mären im Kontext von Minnereden, Bispeln und Romanen. München 1985) geprägt ist. Diese läßt sich offenbar durchaus genauer bestimmen und gegenüber andern Erzählformen wie dem Bîspel, dem Exemplum, Minnereden oder dem Roman abgrenzen. Als Versuch in dieser Richtung versteht sich der Aufsatz von Ch. Ortmann und H. Ragotzky (Zur Funktion exemplarischer *triuwe*-Beweise in Minne-Mären: 'Die treue Gattin' Herrands von Wildonie, 'Das Herzmäre' Konrads von Würzburg und die 'Frauentreue'. in: K. Grubmüller u.a. (Hgg.), Kleinere Erzählformen im MA. Paderborner Colloquium 1987. Paderborn 1988, S. 89-109), in dem sie zu dem Schluß kommen: "Damit wäre prinzipiell nachgewiesen, daß typologische Kriterien des Märes literarisch objektivierbar sind, daß also der Gattungsbegriff Märe keineswegs obsolet ist" (ebd. S. 107). In diesem Sinne halte ich als Arbeitstitel zunächst am Märenbegriff sowie an Fischers Textkorpus fest, um pragmatisch die Art und Funktion der Paardarstellung in diesem Erzähltypus zu befragen.

[2] E. Kartschoke, Kleinepik. in: U. Liebertz-Grün (Hg.), Aus der Mündlichkeit in die Schriftlichkeit: Höfische und andere Literatur. 750-1320. (Deutsche Literatur – Eine Sozialgeschichte, hg.v. H.A. Glaser, Bd. 1) Reinbek 1988, S. 297.

[3] E. Köhler, Einige Thesen zur Literatursoziologie. in: E.K., Vermittlungen. Romanistische

Fall, daß das Märe Fragen stellt, die zu dieser Zeit als aktuell und neu empfunden wurden. Was sind das für Fragen? Richten sie sich auf das Gesellschaftsgefüge insgesamt, also auf die Gewichtung, den Einfluß und die Lebensform des Adels bzw. auf die Trägerschicht der neuen ökonomischen Struktur, die Kaufleute und das Stadtpatriziat? Oder beziehen sie sich spezieller auf Teilaspekte, die in der Märendichtung problematisiert werden?

In den Kern der Mären-Problematik führt, wie eine Gesamtanalyse der Texte zeigt, die Frage, wie das Rollenverständnis des Mannes bzw. der Frau im gesellschaftlichen Zusammenwirken aussieht. Ein Blick auf die Häufigkeit der Paar-Thematik mag das Gewicht dieser Frage unterstreichen. Geht man von Fischers Märenkatalog[4] aus, so zeigt sich, daß in fast genau drei Vierteln aller Texte das Thema der Paarbeziehungen bearbeitet wird.[5] Das restliche Viertel beschäftigt sich mit den unterschiedlichsten sonstigen Phänomenen,[6] die hier beiseite bleiben können. Verglichen damit scheint das Gewicht und die Problematik der Paarbeziehungen für diese Gattung das zentrale Thema zu sein.

Bedrängend wurde diese Frage deshalb, da in Deutschland durch den historischen Territorialisierungsprozeß große Teile des Adels in ihrem Selbsverständnis verunsichert waren und durch das Erstarken der Städte seit dem 13. Jahrhundert, durch eine erweiterte soziale Mobilität sowie durch die Einführung des Römischen Rechts das gesamte Sozialgefüge verändert wurde. Rolle und Funktion des Mannes und der Frau blieben davon nicht unberührt. Was spiegelt sich nun von diesen historischen Vorgängen in den Mären, gesehen in der speziellen Verhaltenstypik eines Paares?

Beiträge zu einer historisch-soziologischen Literaturwissenschaft. München 1976, S. 8-15, hier S. 11 f. These 12.

4   Siehe Anm. 1. Es geht hier nicht darum, die Mären zahlenmäßig vollständig zu erfassen (das führte unausweichlich in die Gattungsdiskussion zurück), sondern ein repräsentatives Textkorpus für die anstehenden Untersuchungen zugrundezulegen. Insofern darf Fischers Katalog als voll ausreichende Textbasis gelten. (Daran ändert auch die Nichteinbeziehung der 44 "Grenzfälle der Märendichtung" [bei H.-J. Ziegeler, Erzählen im Spätmittelalter (wie Anm. 1), S. 495-509] vom Ergebnis her nichts.)

5   Von erfaßten 212 Mären sind dies 158 Texte = 74,5%. Monika Jonas (Der spätmittelalterliche Versschwank. Studien zur Vorform trivialer Literatur. Innsbruck 1987, S. 40 [Innsbrucker Beiträge zur Kulturwissenschaft, Germanist. Reihe, 32]) kommt in einer ähnlichen Statistik, die jedoch nur die 120 Schwankmären erfaßt, auf 103 Texte = 86% der Schwänke unter dem Stichwort "erotische Themen".

6   Loyalität zwischen Ratgeber und Herrscher, zwischen Herr und Knecht; Forderung nach Dankbarkeitserweis für erfahrene Hilfe; Lehrbeispiel zum vierten Gebot zur Achtung der Eltern; aber auch Diebs- und Betrugsgeschichten; Beichtsatiren mit oft generellem Spott über die Pfaffen; eine Reihe von Exkrementenwitzen u.a.

Im folgenden möchte ich dieser Frage in einem Dreischritt nachgehen.

In einem ersten kürzeren Teil betrachten wir den gesellschaftlichen Rahmen, in den sich die Märendichtung stellt. Hier geht es um die ständischen Rahmenbedingungen, die den Handlungsraum eines Paares prägen.

Der zweite Teil beschäftigt sich mit zentralen Themen des Märes, etwa der Form der Ehe, der Darstellung der Frau, aber auch der Normenfrage allgemein.

Der dritte Teil gilt der Bestimmung des Aussagewerts dieser Art Literatur, bezogen auf die historisch zeitgenössischen Realverhältnisse. Wie direkt spiegeln sich die historischen Strukturen in der poetischen Gattung des Märes? Und was läßt sich umgekehrt sozialhistorisch daraus schließen?

I Der Gesellschaftsrahmen

Vor dem Hintergrund einer ständisch gegliederten Gesellschaft ist für die Mären zu erwarten, daß der Vorgang der Paarfindung und die Struktur der typischen Lebensform des Paares standesspezifisch unterschiedlich geprägt sind. Ein genauerer Blick auf die Texte zeigt jedoch, daß diese Vorannahme keineswegs zutrifft. Denn zum einen läßt sich die ständische Zuweisung des Mären-Personals zu den Statusgruppen Ritter/Adel, Bürger (wie immer diese Gruppe genauer zu definieren wäre)[7] und Bauer für viele Mären nicht genau bestimmen. In über 15% aller Fälle (= 25 Paarmären) bleibt die Standeszugehörigkeit unklar. Zum andern zeigt sich, daß in der Thematik der Paarmären die ständisch-personelle Zuordnung in jedem fünften Fall (32 Mären) nicht standesimmanent, sondern ständeübergreifend behandelt wird, d.h. daß zum Beispiel die bekannte Typik von Ritter mit Bürgersfrau oder von Pfaffe mit Bäurin verwendet wird. Diese hierarchische Abwärtsperspektive ist nicht neu, sondern auch in andern Gattungen wie etwa der Pastourelle erzähltypisch. Gewicht erhält diese Feststellung im Märe aber dadurch, daß in Einzelfällen auch die ständische Umkehrung von unten nach oben gestaltet wird, z.B. ein Scholar umwirbt die höherständische Dame,[8] oder – noch einmal als Umkehrung: die hohe Dame bemüht sich um einen nichtadligen Mann.[9]

---

7   Der "Bürger"-Begriff in der Forschungsliteratur dient häufig lediglich der Negativabgrenzung gegenüber dem ritterlichen Adel, dem Klerikerstand und dem Bauernstand. (So z.B. Fischer, Studien [wie Anm. 1] S. 123f.). Insofern umfaßt dieser Begriff zentral die Gruppe der Stadtbewohner, ohne deren soziologische Spannweite (vom Patrizier oder Bürgermeister bis zum Handwerkergesellen oder dem städtischen Knecht) genauer zu differenzieren.

8   "Frauenlist", genauere Angaben bei: H. Fischer, Forschungsbibliographie, Teil B, in: H. Fischer, Studien (wie Anm. 1) Nr. 37. [künftig zitiert als: F].

Vielleicht könnte man sogar noch einen Schritt weitergehen. Denn eine der überraschendsten Beobachtungen an den Texten ist die, daß die Paarprobleme in allen Schichten dieselben zu sein scheinen. So hat der Edelmann mit seiner nach größerer Selbständigkeit strebenden Frau ähnliche Schwierigkeiten wie der Bürger oder Bauer mit seinem widerspenstigen Weib.[10] Oder umgekehrt sucht die adlige Dame dieser Erzählungen genau so wie die Bäurin sexuellen Lustgewinn,[11] gleichgültig, wie der jeweilige ständische Freiraum im einzelnen aussieht. Daraus ergibt sich die Folgerung, daß wir bezüglich des Rollenverhaltens der Geschlechter in den verschiedenen Ständen eine weitgehende Identität feststellen. Das aber bedeutet, daß sich ständisch gerade keine Spezifikation abzeichnet, sondern im Gegenteil Verhaltensmodelle dominieren, die eine gegen die gültigen Normen gerichtete Emanzipationstendenz erkennen lassen. Ob diese Normen die Ehe, die Oberherrschaft des Mannes, oder die Treue der Frau betreffen, – nirgends ist aus ständischer Sicht ein Unterschied herausgehoben. Statt dessen scheint die Fragestellung so allgemeiner Natur zu sein, daß sie grundsätzlich über die Standesschranken hinausweist. Das Problem der Paar-Struktur wird offenbar als ein ständeübergreifendes, allgemein anthropologisches empfunden. Daher zeigen die Erzähler immer wieder allgemein die Verhaltenstypik *des Mannes* bzw. *der Frau.*

Diese sehr allgemeine, gleichsam ahistorische Erzähltypik der deutschen Mären wurde schon früher festgestellt.[12] Ergänzend gehört zu dieser typisierenden Darstellung der Mären aber auch, daß "eine zeitliche Fixierung der Handlung so gut wie nie statt[findet], in einigen wenigen Fällen haben die Schwankpersonen Namen, die aber fast alle weit verbreitet sind und nicht auf die Bezeichnung

---

9   Hans Schneeberger, Der Mönch als Liebhaber C – F 112; Heinrich Kaufringer, Die Rache des Ehemanns – F 67k.

10 Vgl. die Materialzusammenstellung bei F. Brietzmann, Die böse Frau in der deutschen Literatur des Mittelalters. Berlin 1912 (Palaestra 42).

11 Vgl. das breite Spektrum von einschlägigen Textanalysen bei H. Hoven, Studien zur Erotik in der deutschen Märendichtung. Göppingen 1978 (Göppinger Arbeiten zur Germanistik, 256).

12 Hanns Fischer spricht in seiner Untersuchung der ständischen Schichtung des Personals der Mären (Studien [wie Anm. 1] S. 125f.) davon, "daß es keine unantastbaren und ausnahmslos gültigen Rollenprivilegien gibt und daß in gewissem Umfang sogar das Gesetz der Vertauschbarkeit des Personals herrscht". Außerdem erwecke die Darstellung den Anschein, "als werde der soziale Unterschied im Märe nicht in seinen realen Konsequenzen miterlebt" (ebd. S. 125f.); und Monika Jonas (wie Anm. 5, S. 182): "Die Zugehörigkeit zu einem bestimmten sozialen Stand ist für die Figuren im Schwank zunächst von zweitrangiger Bedeutung."

einer bestimmten, individuellen Person abzielen".[13] Für die Rollengestaltung des Personals heißt das, daß sie durch und durch typisch festgelegt ist. Daher hat sich unsere Aufmerksamkeit vor allem darauf zu richten, wie weit sich diese literarische Typik mit andern Typisierungen, z.b. der misogynen Tradition, deckt oder signifikant davon abweicht.

Angesichts der durchgängigen Typisierung ist nun nicht weiter verwunderlich, daß das Märe zwar erkennbar in der mittelalterlich gegliederten Ständegesellschaft angesiedelt ist, daß diese selbst in ihren Unterschieden aber nicht betont wird. Wiederum zahlenmäßig spiegelt sich die historische Entwicklung vom 13. zum 16. Jahrhundert darin insofern, daß von den ständischen Zuweisungen in den Mären des 13. Jahrhunderts das ritterliche Personal dominiert, von der Mitte des 14. Jahrhunderts ab das sog. Bürgertum deutlich zunimmt, die Bauern dagegen insgesamt dahinter zurückbleiben.[14] Vergleicht man dagegen den Personalstatus der Gattung von ca. 1200 bis 1500 insgesamt, so zeigt sich, daß Adlige und Bürger mit jeweils rund 45 Prozent etwa gleich stark vertreten sind, wogegen Bauern nur in rund einem Drittel der Texte begegnen. Diese Zahl überrascht in ihrer Höhe vielleicht. Sie wird aber verständlich, wenn man bedenkt, daß gerade in der klassischen Schwanksituation von Pfaffe und Bäurin der Bauer oft die traditionelle Gegenrolle des Trottels oder Dummkopfs zu vertreten hat.

Innerhalb des allgemeinen Ständepanoramas zeichnen nur wenige Ausnahmen hier ein deutlicheres Bild; so z.B. in Ruprechts von Würzburg "Die zwei Kaufleute" (1. Hälfte 14 Jh.).[15] Darin beschließen zwei führende Handelsherren

---

13 F. Frosch-Freiburg, Schwankmären und Fabliaux. Ein Stoff- und Motivvergleich. Göppingen 1971, S. 233 (Göppinger Arbeiten z. Germanistik, 49). M. Jonas (wie Anm. 5) spricht in diesem Zusammenhang vom Darstellungsverfahren der 'Ubiquität': "Der Schwank schildert Menschen und ihre unterschiedlichen [...] Konfliktsituationen unter dem Aspekt der überzeitlichen Gültigkeit. Das Geschehen ist nicht gebunden an einen bestimmten Ort oder einen bestimmten Zeitpunkt. Er geht davon aus, daß der Mensch ein Wesen mit immer gleichen Eigenschaften und Verhaltensmustern ist. Damit ist [...] die Voraussetzung gegeben für die 'Ubiquität' des Schwanks ..." (S. 187).

14 Diese grobe Tendenzskizze bezieht sich ausschließlich auf das Personal der Mären, soweit deren zeitliche Einordnung überhaupt möglich ist. Sowohl Fischers Beobachtungen zur Ständetypik innerhalb des Märes (Studien [s. Anm. 1] S. 123ff.), wie seine Einschätzung des Märenpublikums mit der leichten ständischen Akzentverschiebung seit dem späteren 14. Jahrhundert auf das städtische Bürgertum hin (ebd. S. 244), wie auch die Ergebnisse der "approximativen" Märendatierung durch H. Hoven (wie Anm. 11; Tabellen der Seiten 36, 115-116; 214-216) und M. Jonas (wie Anm. 5; Ausführungen und Tabellen s. 100-106) ergeben trotz der Ungenauigkeiten im einzelnen doch ein ziemlich übereinstimmendes Bild, das sich mit meinen eigenen Beobachtungen und Vergleichen weitgehend deckt.

15 Bei Fischer (Nr. 108) unter dem Titel: "Die Treueprobe". – Zum folgenden siehe H. Linke, Das Gesellschaftsbild der deutschen Märendichtung. in: Deutsche Literatur des Spätmittel-

von Verdun, durch die Verheiratung ihrer Kinder ihre Hausmachtpolitik im
städtischen Patriziat auszubauen. Diese Entscheidung wird unter dem erklärten
Widerspruch der Ehefrau des Reicheren getroffen, die sich für ihre Tochter
einen Grafen oder Herzog als Ehemann wünscht. Der Kaufmann aber lehnt dies
kategorisch mit dem Hinweis ab, seine Tochter solle später nie den Vorwurf,
daß sie ständisch nicht ebenbürtig sei, erleiden müssen. Aus dem neuen ökonomischen Selbstbewußtsein des Stadtpatriziats leitet sich dann auch ab, daß der
Tugendadel als neue Qualifikation gegen den Geburtsadel gesetzt wird und damit die alte ständisch-ethische Klammer mit ihrer Bevorzugung der Adelsgesell-
schaft in Frage gestellt und zunehmend zurückgedrängt wird. Außerhalb der
Paarthematik zeigen sich denn auch deutlicher sozialkritische Töne wie in Kauf-
ringers "Der verklagte Bauer" (F 67a; vom Ende des 14. Jh.s), wo der kleine
Mann ausdrücklich gegen die Übergriffe der höheren Stände – hier des Pfarrers
und des Richters – verteidigt wird.

II Thematik

Spielt also nach unserer bisherigen Feststellung die eigentlich bedeutsame Rolle
im Märe nicht die Ständegesellschaft als solche, sondern die Paarbeziehung, so
verdeutlich sich die zwischenmenschliche Problematik im nun folgenden Teil
durch die Themen, die abgehandelt werden. Hier sind es vor allem solche, die in
ihrem Verlauf bzw. Ausgang eine Ambivalenz erlauben.

Sehr häufig geht es um das Bedürfnis der sexuellen Lustbefriedigung. Dies ist
ein umfassender Aspekt, der exemplarisch sowohl als Ehebruch wie auch als
voreheliche Geschlechtsbeziehung dargestellt wird.[16] Offen aber ist der Ausgang. Denn sowohl das Gelingen wie das Mißlingen ist möglich und wird dargestellt. Dadurch findet sich der Hörer/Leser in einer gespannten Erwartung,
was die Modifikationen des Themas und auch den Erfolg des Ausbrechers aus
der Norm angeht.

Ähnlich verbreitet ist das Thema der Kraftproben in der Ehe.[17] Hier geht es

alters. Ergebnisse, Probleme und Perspektiven der Forschung. Greifswald 1986 (Deutsche
Literatur des Mittelalters, 3) S. 166-179, hier S. 170f.

[16] Der "Liebhaber" ist hier die Schlüsselfigur, die in rund 64% der Paarmären (100 Texte von
158) begegnet. Dabei ist die außereheliche Lustbefriedigung fast genau doppelt so häufig
dargestellt (66 Mären) wie die voreheliche Geschlechtsbeziehung (34 Texte). – Vgl. dazu
die Nennung und Aufschlüsselung der Schwänke mit Unverheirateten bzw. der Ehebruch-
schwänke bei M. Jonas (wie Anm. 5; S. 48-81).

[17] Vgl. die Aufzählung der Texte und die Analyse der Konstellation bei M. Jonas (wie Anm.

meist um die fraglose Anerkennung der männlichen Oberhoheit gegenüber weiblichen Selbständigkeitsbestrebungen. Offenkundig ist die traditionelle Rollenverteilung hier nicht mehr selbstverständlich akzeptiert, so daß es darüber zum Streit kommt. Der Ausgang ist auch hier wieder ungewiß. So begegnen beide Möglichkeiten: der Typ des bösen Weibes, die ihren Mann total unter der Knute hat, wie umgekehrt die männlich brachiale Gewalt, die schlimmstenfalls die Frau sogar einmauern läßt, bis sie sich bekehrt hat und – als spezielle Form der Ironie – am Ende sogar als Missionarin für die männliche Dominanz werbend durch die Lande reist.[18]

Der Komplementärpart dazu ist die Umkehrung der innerehelichen Fehde: der Treuebeweis der Frau.[19] Er wird dargestellt als durchgehaltene, erprobte, von der Frau fraglos geleistete Treue, aber auch als deren Verweigerung – wieder in der Ambivalenz von erfolgreich oder mißglückt und daher bestraft.

Im Rollenspiel der Geschlechter prägt üblicherweise die Dominanz des Mannes in allen Bereichen – als Vater, als Ehemann wie als Werber – auch im Märe die literarische Typik des Mannes. Insoweit diese Typik durchaus traditionell ist, fällt sie im mittelalterlichen sozialen Kontext auch in der Literatur kaum auf. Wenn die folgende Analyse der einschlägigen Geschehnisse im Märe das genauere Augenmerk jedoch vor allem auf die Figur der Frau richtet,[20] dann deshalb, weil an ihr die von der Tradition abweichenden Neuerungen in dieser Gattung besonders oft und besonders deutlich gezeigt werden. Mit den genannten Themen verdichtet sich die Mären-Perspektive um das Zentrum des Rollenspiels von Mann und Frau, wobei der Ausgang nunmehr völlig offen ist. Daraus kann man schließen, daß die traditionelle Verhaltenstypik für Mann und Frau vom 13. Jahrhundert ab neu problematisiert wird, daß innerhalb der Märendichtung aber selbst am Ende des 15. Jahrhunderts noch keine neue Norm erkennbar ist, nach der die Bewertung von Beziehungen beurteilt würde.

Damit komme ich zur genaueren Betrachtung der Märenthematik im einzelnen. Beginnen wir mit einem Beispiel.

Eine im 15. Jahrhundert offenbar verbreitetere Erzählung unter dem Titel "Die Nachtigall"[21] berichtet folgendes: Ein reicher Ritter hat die Werbung der drei

---

5; S. 85-87).

[18] Der Stricker, Die eingemauerte Frau – F 127g.

[19] Vgl. Texte und Analyse bei M. Jonas (wie Anm. 5; S. 82f.).

[20] Vgl. M. Londner, Eheauffassung und Darstellung der Frau in der spätmittelalterlichen Märendichtung. Eine Untersuchung auf der Grundlage rechtlich-sozialer und theologischer Voraussetzungen. Diss. FU Berlin 1973.

[21] Die Nachtigall B – F 91; danach hier zitiert. (Vgl. dazu die frühere Variante A – F 90). Zur

Söhne eines armen Nachbarn um seine einzige Tochter nicht angenommen. Da
bestellt das Mädchen einen der Söhne nachts zu sich in den Garten, wo es unter
dem Vorwand, nur durch den Gesang der Nachtigall von einer angeblichen
Krankheit gesunden zu können, sein Bett aufgeschlagen hat. Am Morgen findet
der Vater das Paar schlafend im Garten, wobei das Mädchen die "Nachtigall"
seines Geliebten in der Hand hält. Die herbeigerufene Mutter macht dem Mädchen Vorwürfe, aber dieses erwidert, Vögel solcher Art fänden ihren Weg immer auch in die Hände wohlerzogener Jungfrauen. Daraufhin werden die beiden
vermählt.

Dieses bereits von Boccaccio gestaltete Motiv findet bei dem anonymen Autor
aus dem Augsburger oder Nürnberger Raum des 15. Jahrhunderts im Märe hier
eine unüberhörbare sozialkritische Note. Ausgangspunkt ist die Tatsache, daß
der reiche Vater die Werbung der Söhne des armen Nachbarn ablehnt. Die
Zurückweisung der Brautwerbung erfolgt also durchaus traditionell nach stände-
relevanten Prinzipien wie Ansehen und Geld. Die getroffene Entscheidung wird
in diesem Fall von der Tochter allerdings – entgegen den gültigen Normen –
nicht akzeptiert. Jedoch widerspricht sie nicht offen, sondern sie bedient sich
einer List, der vorgespiegelten Krankheit, die durch Vogelgesang im Garten
geheilt werden könne. Der Perspektivenwechsel vom Vater zur Tochter, der hier
mit der Beschreibung der List ansetzt, führt konsequent noch weiter. Aktiv
handelt in diesem Werbungsverfahren nicht der Mann, sondern die liebende
Frau, die auf ihre Weise das festgefahrene juristische Procedere unterläuft. Als
nämlich ihre Eltern die beiden in flagranti ertappen, gibt es juristisch nur die
Alternative: entweder verliert der Vater bei Bekanntwerden des Vorgangs seine
Ehre oder der Jüngling sein Leben. Der Schluß hier lautet aber: einvernehmliche
Heirat.

Was als Epimythion vom Erzähler angefügt ist, trifft den Kern der unter-
schwelligen Kritik wie so oft nur halb: Wer eine erwachsene Tochter habe,
möge sie möglichst rasch verheiraten. – Interessanterweise sind hier sämtliche
entscheidenden, neueren kritischen Aspekte aus der Moralanwendung ausge-
klammert worden, nämlich die Sozialkritik an der Überbewertung von Geld sowie die Bewunderung des lachend vorgetragenen Sieges der List über die Norm,
deren Ergebnis am Ende auch der gesellschaftsbewußte Vater akzeptieren muß.

Während diese Erzählung bei Boccaccio und weitgehend noch in der ersten in
Deutschland überlieferten Textversion aus dem 14./15. Jahrhundert[22] lediglich
die Transposition eines bekannten erotischen Motivs[23] ins ritterliche Milieu und

---

Datierung und zur Quelle: H.J. Ziegeler, in: Verfasserlexikon[2] Bd. 6 (1987) Sp. 843-845.

[22] Die Version A: Fischer Nr. 90.

[23] Vgl. die Metapher: "die Nachtigall fangen" für den Koitus. Motiv- und Textnachweise bei

ein Exemplum für das Liebesglück trotz äußerer Widerstände war, hat sich der erzählerische Skopus im Lauf des 15. Jahrhunderts verschoben. Akzentuiert ist jetzt die listige Frau sowie die Tatsache, daß die väterliche Aufsicht mit gutem Grund unterlaufen wird. Die Minne ist nur noch der Anlaß für die betrügerische Inszenierung, aber nicht mehr deren Begründung.

Der Hintergrund dieser im Schwank vermittelten Kritik ist die Tatsache, daß die patriarchalische Gesellschaftsstruktur noch immer als Norm gilt, sie von verschiedenen Seiten aber in Frage gestellt wird. An zwei Themenkomplexen vor allem wird das verdeutlicht: Einmal an der Ehebruchthematik, die sich nicht primär als Gesetzesübertretung durch Verletzung der Rechte des Ehemannes oder als moralisches Vergehen darstellt, sondern als eine zurecht erfolgende Liebeserfüllung nach den Wünschen der Frau. Dasselbe gilt analog für die voreheliche Umgehung der Rechtsaufsicht des Vaters durch die Tochter, wodurch sie sich den nach eigener Entscheidung gewählten Mann selbständig nimmt. Gemeinsam ist beiden Märenthemen, daß sich die Gestaltungstendenz fast nie primär gegen die männlichen Vorrechte richtet, als vielmehr für die Eigenständigkeit der Frau und ihre freie Entscheidung eintritt. Rein quantitativ zeigt sich dabei wieder, daß sich diese Frage mit rund 70 Prozent der Paarmären in weit größerem Umfang auf die innereheliche Problematik richtet, als auf die voreheliche mit nur knapp 30 Prozent. Allerdings ist bei der letztgenannten Textgruppe nicht zu übersehen, daß sich dort jene Tendenz der Antinorm fast ganz auf die freie weibliche Wahl eines Liebhabers konzentriert.

Der *voreheliche* Spielraum der Begegnung der Frau mit einem Mann wird im Märe in einer vielfältigen Breite von Situationen vor Augen geführt. Während beispielsweise männliche Werbungen mit dem ausschließlichen Ziel von Liebesabenteuern[24] und die zuweilen raffinierte Übertölpelung von naiven Mädchen[25] durchaus im Erwartungshorizont der Zeit liegen, richtet sich die Aufmerksamkeit des Erzählers überraschend oft auf die aktive Frau. Während sich etwa die hübsche Phyllis in der bekannten Geschichte von Aristoteles und Phyllis[26] für die Verhinderung ihrer Liebe zu Alexander am Philosophen rächt, kann sich der Zorn der Frau genauso auf den Liebhaber richten, wenn er sie nach dem Liebesgenuß einfach verlassen will. (Im "Nonnenturnier" etwa sorgt sie auf sublime Weise dafür, daß sich der Mann selbst kastriert.)[27] Andererseits kann die

---

Ziegeler, Verfasserlexikon² Bd. 6 (1987) Sp. 843.

24 Hans Volz, Drei Studenten – F 122.

25 Das Häslein – F 50; Der Sperber – F 125. Zur Textgruppe: "sexuelle Unerfahrenheit/Verführung" siehe M. Jonas (wie Anm. 5; S. 47).

26 Fischer Nr. 6.

weibliche Abwehr der Sexualität nach deren erster realer Erfahrung bei der Frau aber auch in Genuß umschlagen, so daß sie nicht mehr genug davon bekommen kann.[28]

In dieser Textgruppe verdichten sich, wie angedeutet, drei Bereiche mit ganz unterschiedlicher Tendenz. 1. Traditionsgemäß finden sich hier Frauen als Opfer der Liebeslust von Männern. Diese Schänder weiblicher Ehre müssen bestraft werden, selbst wenn es dabei um die höchstrichterliche Rechtfertigung des dreifachen Mordes durch eine dreimal vergewaltigte Gräfin geht.[29] 2. Abweichend von der Erwartung ist jedoch, daß sich die Frauen keineswegs als Opfer vorkommen, sondern sie durchaus Freude am sexuellen Genuß haben, ja, daß sie diesen sogar mit allen Mitteln auch für die Zukunft sichern wollen. Ist ein Liebhaber dazu nicht bereit, muß er mit der Rache der Dame rechnen. – In dieser Gruppe ist weniger ein typisch weibliches Verhalten gestaltet, als wohl eher eine typisch männliche Projektion, wie man die Frau in ihrem Sexualverhalten gerne hätte: nämlich jederzeit zum Verkehr bereit, schamlos und unersättlich. Die 3. Gruppe ist die weitaus umfangreichste. Sie präsentiert die listenreiche aktive Frau, die alle Möglichkeiten ausschöpft, um zum jeweils ersehnten Ziel zu kommen. Das kann genau so der gezielte Erwerb eines Mannes nach Wahl der Frau sein,[30] oder echte Liebeserfüllung[31] wie auch der Wunsch nur nach sexueller Vereinigung.[32]

Mit der listenreichen Frau aber ist auch die Klammer gegeben, die zur *Eheproblematik* hinüberführt. Ob verheiratet oder nicht, ob Mann oder Frau, mit dem faszinierenden Spiel der raffiniert angewandten Intelligenz scheint *das* zentrale Gestaltungsmittel der Mären angesprochen.[33] Spätestens hier wird deut-

---

[27] Fischer Nr. 93.

[28] Johannes von Freiberg, Das Rädlein – F 64; Der verklagte Zwetzler – F 148.

[29] Heinrich Kaufringer, Die unschuldige Mörderin – F 67i.

[30] Der Mönch als Liebesbote A, B, C – F 86/67h/112.

[31] Der Schüler zu Paris – F 118-120 (mit dem gemeinsamen Liebestod nach Liebesglück); Die Nachtigall A, B – F 90-91.

[32] Die verspotteten Liebhaber – F 78.

[33] Auffällig ist die Häufigkeit der Verwendung von *list* in den Mären. In 78,5% der Texte (absolut: 124 von 158) ist eine List das handlungsbestimmende Motiv, wobei der größere Anteil den Frauen zufällt (48%). Allerdings verschleiert der Gebrauch von List und Gegenlist (Männer 42%) die weibliche Dominanz etwas. – Vgl. S.L. Wailes, Stricker and the Virtue 'Prudentia': A Critical Review. in: Seminar 13 (1977), S. 136-153; H. Ragotzky, Das Handlungsmodell der *list* und die Thematisierung der Bedeutung von *guot*. Zum Problem einer sozialgeschichtlich orientierten Interpretation von Strickers "Daniel vom blühenden Tal" und dem "Pfaffen Amis". in: Literatur, Publikum, historischer Kontext. Hg. v. G. Kaiser. Bern/Frankfurt 1977, S. 183-302 (Beiträge zur älteren deutschen Litera-

lich, daß die Paarproblematik nunmehr unter neuen Bedingungen reflektiert wird. Mehrheitlich akzeptiert sind nicht mehr die überkommenen Rollenfestlegungen vom übergeordneten Mann und der untergeordneten, gehorsamen Frau, noch werden die dementsprechenden Züchtigungsmittel wie Prügel oder Strafandrohungen bejaht. Sondern gesucht werden neue Normen aufgrund eines neuen Rollen- und Identitätsverständnisses.

Die neue Begründungsbasis beruht einerseits auf dem Leistungsgedanken, und in unmittelbarer Beziehung damit auf der Frage von Kenntnissen oder Fähigkeiten. Beide Bereiche sind überall dort gefordert und notwendig, wo die alte geburtsrechtlich geregelte Ständestruktur ineffektiv geworden ist und durch andere Qualifikationen ersetzt werden muß. Das ist im gesamten ökonomischen Bereich mit der Umstellung auf die frühen Kapitalstrukturen der Fall, das gilt aber nicht minder für den neuen bürgerlichen Bildungsanspruch, der seit dem beginnenden 13. Jahrhundert in breiter Front auch die sogenannten "Laien"[34] erfaßt. Einige namentlich faßbare Märendichter wie der Stricker (1. Hälfte 13. Jh.), Hans Rosenplüt (Anf. 15. Jh. – ca. 1460) oder Hans Folz (ca. 1435-1513) sind uns zugleich bekannt als Autoren von bildungsmäßig höchst anspruchsvoller Spruch- oder Lehrdichtung. Insofern ist es nicht verwunderlich, daß bei dieser Textgattung der Mären die intellektuelle Leistungsfähigkeit in über drei Vierteln aller Erzählungen thematisiert ist. List, Raffinesse, geistige Überlegenheit spielen unter den menschlichen Qualitäten dieser Texte die ausschlaggebende Rolle. Bemerkenswert daran ist, daß die Umwertung in vollem Umfang auch die Frau erfaßt und daß die neue Ebene der ehelichen Auseinandersetzungen nun der Kopf statt der Faust ist. Diese zentrale Verlagerung soll uns etwas genauer beschäftigen.

Frauenlist innerhalb der Ehe wird in über der Hälfte aller Fälle durch das Dreiecksverhältnis mit einem Liebhaber aktiviert. Ihre Bemühungen sind darauf gerichtet, einen Liebhaber zu erwerben, ihn sodann zu erhalten und ihn schließlich zu verteidigen gegen Entdeckung. Dabei ist den weiblichen Bemühungen in den meisten Fällen Erfolg beschieden. Diese listige Dreieckssicherung findet ihre erzählerische Steigerung darin, daß sich zum Beispiel gleich drei buhle-

turgeschichte, 1).

34 Siehe G. Steer, Zum Begriff "Laie" in deutscher Dichtung und Prosa des Mittelalters. in: Literatur und Laienbildung im Spätmittelalter und in der Reformationszeit. Symposion Wolfenbüttel 1981. Hg. v. L. Grenzmann – K. Stackmann, Stuttgart 1984, S. 764-768 (Germanist. Symposien. Berichtsbände, 5); ders., Der Laie als Anreger und Adressat deutscher Prosaliteratur im 14. Jahrhundert. in: Zur deutschen Literatur und Sprache des 14. Jahrhunderts. Dubliner Colloquium 1981. Hg. v. W. Haug u.a., Heidelberg 1983, S. 354-367 (Reihe Siegen, Germ. Abt., 45).

rische Frauen[35] gegenseitig zu überbieten suchen und als zusätzlichen Anreiz eine Belohnung für diejenige aussetzen, die ihren Mann am besten betrügen kann. Gemeinsam soll dann über die drei Fälle entschieden werden.

So berichtet die erste, daß sie am Freitag beim Fischebraten von ihrem Buhlen entführt wurde und eine Woche von zu Hause fort war. Am Freitag darauf stand sie plötzlich wieder vor dem Herd und machte ihrem Mann weis, er sei während des Fischebratens eingeschlafen. Die zweite erzählt, sie habe ihren mißtrauischen Mann davon überzeugt, daß sie mit der "Nachtfrau ausfahren" müsse. Nachdem sie bis zum Morgen mit dem Geliebten im Garten zusammen war, wartete ihr einfältiger Mann mit einer Leuchte unter der Haustür auf sie, damit sie bei der Rückkehr nicht stolpere. Die dritte schließlich berichtet von einem Geheimgang, der ihr Schlafzimmer mit dem Haus des Geliebten verband. Als der Mann sie einmal bei jenem Ritter entdeckte, eilte sie schleunigst durch den Gang nach Hause, so daß der das Ehebett prüfende Gatte beim Auffinden seiner dort schlafenden Frau an seinem eigenen Verstand zweifeln mußte. Da sich die drei Frauen nicht einigen konnten, wer den Preis erhalten solle, überläßt der Erzähler das Urteil dem Leser.

In diesem Text ist eines der Erzählprinzipien der Mären deutlich ausgesprochen, die Unterhaltung des Lesers durch Übersteigerung. Daß dabei gerade die ungewöhnlichsten Situationen auch als die witzigsten empfunden werden, weil gerade sie den listigen Erfindungsreichtum am meisten provozieren, ist deutlich. So spielen, um die Witz- und Unterhaltungssituation voll auszureizen, öfters die Frauen der Erzählungen auch die Angst des beinahe ertappten Liebhabers aus, um die Entdeckung im letzten Moment doch noch abzubiegen. Beispielsweise lieben sich eines Abends ein Ritter und eine Bürgersfrau,[36] aber diese Liebschaft wird dem Gatten verraten. Er kommt vorzeitig nach Hause, so daß der Liebhaber nur noch nackt, wie er ist, unter einen Zuber fliehen kann. Der Ehemann mit seinen vier Brüdern lassen sich nun ausgerechnet auf jenem Zuber zum Vesper nieder, unter dem der Ritter liegt. Als einer von ihnen auf den Gedanken kommt, unter dem Zuber hätten sie noch nicht gesucht, fordert die Frau sie so heftig auf, dort zu suchen, daß alle Beteiligten fürchten, sich bei einem Mißerfolg zu blamieren und sie so die Suche bleiben lassen. Aber noch einmal wird das weibliche Spiel mit der Angst erneuert, als die Nachbarin kommt und diesen ihren Zuber zurückverlangt. Erst durch die listige Auskunft der Frau, eine "weibliche Notlage" mache augenblicklich die Rückgabe unmöglich, versteht die Nachbarin den Zusammenhang und zündet zur Hilfe eine Scheune an, damit der

---

35   Drei buhlerische Frauen – F 35.

36   Jacob Appet, Der Ritter unter dem Zuber – F 5.

nackte Ritter in dem ausbrechenden Wirrwarr sich endlich ungesehen davonma-
chen kann. Solche Modelltypik wiederholt sich in zahllosen Fällen, immer mit der
Gewichtung auf der intellektuell überlegenen und die Handlung lenkenden Frau.
Bemerkenswert ist, daß sich das Kräftemessen in der Ehe ebenfalls auf die
List-Ebene verlagert. Männerlist und Frauenlist belauern sich gegenseitig;[37]
zuweilen ergänzt sich aber auch das Partnerspiel mit der Angst um die Note der
Gegenseitigkeit, so daß am Ende die Rechnung offen bleibt, wer den andern
mehr geängstigt habe, der Geliebte die Frau oder umgekehrt.[38]

Untersucht man in einem weiteren Schritt die auffällige Häufigkeit der aktiven
Frauenrolle in den Erzählungen etwas genauer, so zeigt sich, daß es dabei
weniger um die Figur der Frau als solcher geht. Vielmehr dient sie den Autoren
als scharf profiliertes Mittel der Erzählung für eine kritische Durchleuchtung von
gesellschaftlich relevanten Fragen. Im Mittelpunkt steht dabei immer die Brüchig-
keit von Normen, die am veränderten Verhalten der Frau gezeigt wird. Was bislang so sicher in Gesetze, moralische Normen oder einfach gesellschaftliche
Konventionen eingebettet schien, soll nun – zumindest in diesen Erzählungen –
nicht mehr unbedingt gelten. Gesetz und Moral sind brüchig geworden. Daher
spielen diese Frauenfiguren im Märe den ganzen neuen Freiraum, der sich ihnen
realhistorisch andeutungsweise geöffnet hat, nun poetisch experimentell durch.
Daher greift man zu kurz, wenn man die Frauenfigur im Märe nur als Frau von
ihrer traditionellen Rolle her interpretiert und die allgemein gesellschaftlichen
Implikationen dabei übersieht. Thematisch erhält dabei eine andere Motivik eine
fast gleich gewichtige Funktion wie die neue Intellektualität: es sind die
Emotionen, die subjektiven Wünsche und die Triebhaftigkeit der Frau, die in
drastischer Verdeutlichung exemplarisch meist im Kontext der Sexualität vor
Augen geführt werden.[39] Die Engführung dieses Bezugshorizonts für den
Gesamtrahmen deutet an, daß es dabei nicht eigentlich um jene ermüdende
Wiederholung des Spiels mit dem Tabubereich geht. Sondern innerhalb dieser
von der Grundstruktur stets ähnlichen Szenen geht es um unterschiedliche
Gesellschaftsfragen, die sich im Rollenverhalten der Frau zugespitzt spiegeln.

Als Beispiel will ich dies an drei Bereichen zeigen, die sich allesamt auf die
Gliederung, auf fixierte Ansprüche und auf Wertungen der Gesamtgesellschaft
beziehen. Es sind dies
1. die Demontage des Adels und der höfischen Normvorstellungen;

---

37 Der Pfaffe mit der Schnur A, B, C – F 95/4e/96.
38 Heinrich Kaufringer, Chorherr und Schusterin – F 67c.
39 D. Blamires, Sexual comedy in the Mären of Hans Rosenplüt. in: Trivium 11 (1976), S.
90-113; H. Hoven, Studien zur Erotik (wie Anm. 11).

2. die Aushöhlung des ständischen Ehrbegriffs; und
3. die Verschiebung des Ungleichgewichts im Werbungsprozeß zugunsten der
   Frau durch die Legitimierung ihrer Forderung nach Erfüllung von Vorbedingungen.

In allen genannten Fällen ist die Frau also, wie gesagt, nicht eigentlich eine
autonome Figur, sondern nur Funktionsträger für übergeordnete Fragen. Betrachten wir nun die genannten Bereiche.

Ad 1: Demontage des Adels und der höfischen Normvorstellungen. Bei der in
zwei Varianten vorliegenden Erzählung von der "Halben Birne"[40] gehts es
vordergründig um das ungeheure triebhafte Verlangen einer Prinzessin nach Erfüllung ihrer sexuellen Bedürfnisse, wobei sie bereit ist, ihr gesellschaftliches
Ansehen und sogar ihr Leben aufs Spiel zu setzen. Die Art und Weise, wie sich
dieser Vorgang vollzieht, wird besonders dadurch dem ridiculum ausgesetzt,
daß eben diese Königstochter zuvor den besten Turnierritter, der um ihre Hand
geworben hatte, wegen eines Etikettenfehlers bei Tisch in aller Öffentlichkeit
wiederholt verlacht und geschmäht hat. Eine Steigerung geradezu zur Groteske
ergibt sich dadurch, daß genau dieser geschmähte Ritter unerkannt in einer Ver-
kleidung als stummer Narr zum exzessiven Zielpunkt des Sexualverlangens der
so etikettenbetonten Prinzessin wird. Um zum Orgasmus zu kommen, wirft sie
alle Rücksichten moralischer Art und sogar jede Form des Anstands über Bord,
um am darauffolgenden Tag mit hocherhobenem Haupt ihre Schmähung des
Ritters erneut aufzunehmen. Doch als dieser genau so öffentlich die wörtliche
Stimulieraufforderung der Prinzessin aus der Kammer als Antwort zurückgibt,
erschrickt die Frau so, daß sie den Ritter aus Furcht vor der öffentlichen Schan-
de sofort zur Ehe nimmt. Das Epimythion richtet sich scharf gegen die Lüsternheit der Frauen, zumal der Ritter all seiner Verdienste verlustig gegangen wäre,
wenn er sich selbst nicht zuvor zum Narren gemacht hätte.

Die drastische Ausführlichkeit, in der die Begierlichkeit dieser adligen Dame
beschrieben wird, kontrastiert extrem mit dem normativen theoretischen Verhal-
tensmodell, das gesellschaftlich wie moralisch für diesen Stand gilt. Würde sich
eine Bäurin so benehmen, dann deckte sich deren Verhalten mit der öffentlichen
Einschätzung. Erzählerisch wird die Triebhaftigkeit der Prinzessin dadurch noch
verstärkt, daß die vergleichsweise kleine Mißachtung der Tischsitte durch den
Ritter mit der totalen Unmoral der hohen Dame kontrastiert wird. Auch wenn
das Epimythion das Gegensatzpaar von weiblicher *lekerheit* (= Lüsternheit) und
ritterlicher *tugende* nicht bereits negativ herausgestellt hätte, wäre das Verhalten

---

40 Die halbe Birne A – F 74; Hans Folz, Die halbe Birne B – F 30c.

einer hochadligen Dame allein schon durch den öffentlichen Vortrag einer sol-
chen Erzählung diskreditiert.

Den eigentlichen Schlüssel der Aussage finden wir aber erst in der verglei-
chenden Gattungstypik. Die Verdichtung der Komik in diesem Text schlägt immer deutlicher in Parodie um. Parodiertes Muster ist der ritterliche Minnedienst
und die distanziert anbetende Verehrung der Minnedame im hohen Minnesang.[41]
Bereits um die Mitte des 13. Jahrhunderts begegnen im sog. Gegensang, z.b.
bei Geltar oder dem Tannhäuser, Parodien auf diese idealtypische Absolut-
setzung der Frau, von der sich die adlige Männerwelt die eigene vollkommene
ethische Prägung sowie die der ganzen Gesellschaft erhofft. Die Dame ist das
personifizierte erzieherische Leitbild, das sich in jeder höfischen Dame konkreti-
siert. Dieses Modell aber existierte nur in der Poesie, nicht in der Wirklichkeit.
Als Leitbild aber hat der hier artikulierte Anspruch auch als Utopie eine real an-
zustrebende Zielfunktion.

In dem gegen Endes des 13. Jahrhunderts verfaßten Märentext von der "Halben Birne" aber wird gerade jene Zielprojektion karikiert. Zwei literarische Mittel, die schon seit der Jahrhundertmitte dafür gebraucht werden, sind hier mit-
einander kombiniert, 1. die poetisch fiktive Aussage wird erzählerisch wörtlich
genommen. Damit springt die Diskrepanz von Dichtung und Alltagswirklichkeit
in die Augen. Da man aber von der Alltagswirklichkeit aus mißt, wird die
Fiktion in ihrem geistigen Wirklichkeitsanspruch lächerlich gemacht (z.B. der
poetische Minnedienst als eine Form der Distanzliebe, die die Männer bei realer
Begegnung mit der vielbesungenen Frau unfähig macht, ihr einen Kuß zu
geben, geschweige denn noch mehr mit ihr zu tun;[42] oder Leistungsforderun-
gen der Dame an den Ritter, die als Adynata formuliert werden: z.B. wolle sie
nur noch die kleine Bitte von ihm erfüllt bekommen, daß er die Sandkörner auf
dem Meeresgrund zähle, dann wolle sie ihm ganz gehören.[43] Das 2. Mittel ist
das Aufzeigen der Diskrepanz von Anspruch und Wirklichkeit, von behaupteter
Autorität und wirklichem Sachverhalt.

Unser Text verbindet beides, indem er darstellerisch zunächst das idealtypische Bild einer adligen Dame zeigt, das sich im Erzählverlauf aber total umkehrt.
Diesem Kontrast steht der andere zur Seite, welcher vor allem in der zweiten

---

41 Vgl. W. Blank, Deutsche Minnesang-Parodien. in: Poesie und Gebrauchsliteratur im
    deutschen Mittelalter. Würzburger Colloquium 1978. Hg. v. V. Honemann – K. Ruh – B.
    Schnell – W. Wegstein, Tübingen 1979, S. 205-218, bes. S. 213 ff.

42 Vgl. Gedrut/Geltar, Lied Ia, bes. Str. 2; in: Deutsche Liederdichter des 13. Jahrhunderts,
    hg. v. Carl von Kraus, Bd. I, Tübingen 1952, S. 77.

43 Der Tannhäuser, Lied Nr. X, hg. v. Johannes Siebert. in: J.S., Der Dichter Tannhäuser.
    Leben – Gedichte – Sage. Halle/Salle 1934, S. 113-115, hier Verse 8ff.

Textversion von Hans Folz (15. Jh.) herausgestellt wird, in welcher erklärt wird, weshalb der gute Ritter Defizienzen in der Etikette hat: er stammt gar nicht aus dem Geburtsadel, sondern er war nur besonders kampftüchig. Durch seinen ruhmvollen kämpferischen Einsatz im Hl. Land aber wurde er nachträglich geadelt. Spätestens in der Bearbeitung von Folz wird die bislang nur innerliterarisch vergleichende Ständekritik auch nach außen deutlich greifbar.

Die Aussage lautet nun: Zwischen Anspruch und Wirklichkeit des Adels besteht eine große Kluft. Weder ist die adlige Dame in der Lage, das nun als Utopie eingestufte positive Leitbild zu verkörpern, da sie sich moralisch und im normalen Anstandsverhalten schlimmer benimmt als jedes Gassenweib. Noch ist zum andern der Adel bereit, von seiner ständischen Arroganz gegenüber den nicht Gleichrangigen abzurücken. Auch diese Aussage wird an der Figur der Frau verdeutlicht, allerdings unterschiedlich. Die erste Textfassung aus dem 13. Jahrhundert macht das Fehlverhalten an der Diskrepanz des kleinen männlichen Fehlers aus dem Bereich der Tischmanieren gegenüber dem völlig ungezügelten Triebverhalten der Frau im Bett mit ihrer Unmoral deutlich. Die zweite Fassung von Folz zeigt das Fehlverhalten des Adels am sozialen Werdegang des Ritters, der als Person auch nach der Adelung nicht als ebenbürtig betrachtet wird.

Dieses Textbeispiel zeigt, daß das exemplarisch vorgeführte Verhalten einer Dame im Märe – ich erinnere hier noch einmal an die ausgeprägte Figurentypik – dazu geschaffen ist, sowohl das literarische Gegenbild der hohen Minneherrin des Minnesangs zu karikieren, wie andererseits zum grundsätzlichen Nachdenken anzuregen, ob die Verhaltensnormen des Adels von innen her wirklich noch erfüllt sind. Man mag auch in diesem Text auf ganz unerwartete Weise die schon angesprochene Ablösung des Geburtsadels durch den nichtständischen Tugendadel wiederfinden.

– Die beiden andern Bereiche werde ich nur kurz ansprechen.

Ad 2: Die Aushöhlung des ständischen Ehrbegriffs.

Auch diese Behauptung mag durch ein Beispiel verdeutlicht werden. Ein Scholar[44] entbrennt in Liebe zu einer Dame, der er ihres hohen Standes wegen seine Zuneigung zunächst nicht zu bekennen wagt. Nach mehrfachen Gruß- und Annäherungsversuchen formuliert er in einem kurzen Gespräch mit ihr einen Vergleich vom Vogelfang, den sie nicht versteht. Sie bittet ihn um Erklärung, was die Aussage bedeute. Der sich daran anschließende höchst gelehrte und kunstvolle Disput erlaubt dem Scholaren, ihr seine Liebe zu erklären. In mehrfachen Treffen gelingt es ihm schließlich, mit seinen Argumenten ihren

---

[44] Frauenlist – F 37.

Verstand und mit der Wärme seiner Beteuerungen ihr Herz zu überzeugen. So erwidert sie seine Liebe, da die Minne über Gut und Ehre stehe.

Die hier gezeigte Macht der Minne über die höfische Ehre, d.h. über die ständisch-gesellschaftliche Normierung, steht spätestens seit den verschiedenen Tristan- und Lancelot-Bearbeitungen (seit dem Ende des 12. Jahrhunderts) literarisch auf der Tagesordnung. Insofern ist die Gestaltung der vorgetragenen Erzählung thematisch nichts Neues. Sie bestätigt nur noch einmal den alten Satz des "amor vincit omnia". Bemerkenswert ist diese Geschichte aber deshalb, da die Minne im Unterschied zum höfischen Roman hier Standesschranken überschreitet. Die adlige Dame vereint sich schließlich nach einem Dialog mit dem Herzen und nach Überwindung ihrer Bedenken bezüglich ihrer Ehre mit dem Scholaren. "Über allem lagert", wie Karl-Heinz Schirmer beobachtet,[45] "eine feine Ironie im Umgang mit höfischen Traditionen. Sie zeigen sich auch [...] in der Kunst der Redegewandtheit, mit der der Student seine soziale Inferiorität kompensiert und die er in den Dienst der Verführung stellt [...], sowie in Gedanken aus der Minnetheorie, ohne daß dies aber noch ernst genommen würde."

Bestätigt wird dieses Zurücktreten des Ehreaspekts gegenüber der persönlichen Liebe durch ein zweites Beispiel, in dem selbst eine religiös gestützte Tabuverletzung zugunsten der Liebe in Kauf genommen wird. In der Erzählung vom "Falschen Messias"[46] führt die heimliche Liebe eines christlichen Studenten zu einem Judenmädchen zu einer unbeabsichtigten Schwangerschaft. Während die ehrlich gemeinte Brautwerbung noch vor Entdeckung der Schwangerschaft von der Familie des Mädchens sehr grundsätzlich mit massiven religiösen Argumenten abgelehnt wird, wird mit der Aufdeckung der Schwangerschaft selbst diese unerlaubte Tabuverletzung aus Glaubensgründen als vergleichsweise geringeres Übel eingestuft.

Beide Beispiele für das Fehlverhalten einer Frau stellen sich somit als eine sehr viel grundsätzlichere Kritik an Gesellschaftsverhältnissen dar. Dabei läuft der Kernpunkt der Kritik nicht auf eine ständisch determinierte Auseinandersetzung hinaus, sondern sie zielt im Prinzip auf eine Neubewertung der Spannung zwischen Anspruch und Erfüllung durch Qualität. Konkret ist damit genau so die traditionelle Höherbewertung der geburtsständischen Gliederung wie die starre Fixierung der religiös gültigen Normen in Frage gestellt.

Ad 3: Die Verschiebung des Ungleichgewichts im Werbungsprozeß zugunsten der Frau durch die Legitimierung ihrer Forderung nach Erfüllung von Vorbedingungen.

---

45 Verfasserlexikon[2] Bd. 2 (1980), Sp. 864f.

46 Hans Folz, Der falsche Messias – F 30m.

Hier geht es um den prinzipiellen Abbau des männlichen Übergewichts der Rechte zugunsten der Frau. Gerade im Eherecht war die Frau als Folge der Konzeption der alten Stammesrechte noch im 13. Jahrhundert häufig der sogenannten Muntehe unterworfen.[47] Dies hatte die praktische Konsequenz, daß die Frau vor der Eheschließung weder zur Akzeptanz des Partners gefragt wurde, noch daß sie ihre Zustimmung zur Ehe überhaupt geben mußte, noch daß sie irgendwie an der Verhandlung über persönliche oder materielle Ausstattung in der Ehe beteiligt wurde. Mit der Einführung des Römischen Rechts in Deutschland im Lauf des 13. Jahrhunderts, das auch die Kirche in diesem Punkt mit der consensus-Forderung für sich übernahm, ändert sich die Situation zwar theoretisch, in der Praxis dauert es aber noch gute zwei Jahrhunderte, bis der Persönlichkeit der Frau personale Rechte selbstverständlich zugebilligt werden.

An diesem Punkt setzen einige Mären an, in denen die Frau entschieden auf ihren eigenen Vorstellungen, was die Auswahl des Mannes angeht, besteht. So fordert sie als Vorbedingung ihrer Zustimmung zur Vereinigung mit dem Mann entweder bestimmte Turnierleistungen,[48] das Bestehen gezielter Liebesproben,[49] intellektuelle Leistungen[50] oder auch das Vorhandensein bestimmter Körpereigenschaften.[51] Gemeinsam ist der ganzen Textgruppe, daß die Berechtigung solcher Forderungen der Frau prinzipiell nicht in Frage gestellt wird, wenn auch deren Durchführung variiert von weiblicher Willkür und Bosheit bis zur begründeten neuen Idealtypik. Verdeutlicht wird dadurch, daß hier spielerisch Möglichkeiten der neuen Rollentypik der Frau ausgelotet werden, die bis dahin literarisch nur partiell neu reflektiert waren.

III Aussage des Märes

Im dritten Teil versuche ich, die verschiedenen Teilergebnisse, die wir bisher gewonnen haben, in einer Synthese zusammenzufassen. Auszugehen ist dabei

---

[47] W. Ogris, Munt, Muntwalt. in: Handwörterbuch zur deutschen Rechtsgeschichte, hg. v. A. Erler – E. Kaufmann, Bd. III, Berlin 1984, Sp. 750-761; P. Mikat, Ehe. in: ebd., Bd. 1, Berlin 1971, Sp. 809-843, bes. Sp. 810ff.

[48] Die halbe Birne A, B – F 74/30c; Konrad von Würzburg, Der Schwanritter – F 73c; Moriz von Craûn – F 87.

[49] Aristoteles und Phyllis – F 6; Fröschel v. Leidnitz, Die Liebesprobe – F 42; Die verspotteten Liebhaber – F 78; Hans Folz, Die drei Studenten – F 30q.

[50] Heinz der Kellner, Konni – F 58.

[51] Der Preller – F 97; Der Striegel – F 128.

von der Tatsache, daß die Figurenrollen von Mann und Frau im Märe durchgehend stark typisiert sind. Ergänzend ist festzuhalten, daß die jeweilige ständische Zuordnung des Personals zwar für das relative Erzählkolorit notwendig ist, nicht aber für die Tendenz der Gesamtaussage.

Daraus ist der Schluß zu ziehen, daß die behandelten Fragen und Problemlösungen zwar oft innerständisch dargestellt sind, jedoch überständische Gültigkeit besitzen. Das bedeutet, daß die Rollenproblematik von Mann und Frau hier grundsätzlicher Natur ist und als anthropologisches Problem verstanden wird.

Die konkrete Befragung der Mären auf ihren historischen Hintergrund ist ein weiterer Punkt. Sie ergibt, daß dieser Hintergrund nur selten in seiner einmaligen Unverwechselbarkeit angesprochen wird. Insofern ist die Zuordnung von Texten nach Nord- oder Süddeutschland oder ins benachbarte Ausland sowie die zeitliche Fixierung auf das 13. oder 15. Jahrhundert nur von relativer Bedeutung. Das zwingt zu der Schlußfolgerung, daß die Erzählgattung Märe nicht unmittelbar realhistorische Fakten abbildet, sondern daß sie diese nur als Skizzenentwurf und als Kulisse für eine poetisch-literarische, d.h. fiktive Darstellung des menschlichen Verhaltens benutzt. Dies ist besonders wichtig für die Beurteilung einer vermeintlich neuen Funktion der Frau und ihres veränderten, hier gezeigten gesellschaftlichen Stellenwerts. Wenn diese veränderten Verhaltensmodelle der Gesellschaft im Märe also keine unmittelbare Spiegelung der Realität darstellen, ist um so dringlicher zu fragen, was diese neue Typik als Fiktion dann für eine politische Funktion hat.

Bevor wir in der Lage sind, diese wichtige Frage zu beantworten, ist eine letzte literarische Beobachtung zu erwähnen. Es ist bemerkenswert, daß die durchgängige Erzählstruktur der Mären zwei Prinzipien folgt: 1. der erschließbaren Forderung, daß jede Situation und jedes Verhalten so zu gestalten ist, daß der Ausgang bis zuletzt offen bleibt. Ob eine Werbung also gelingt oder ein Ehebruch entdeckt wird, entscheidet sich erzählerisch immer erst am Schluß. Diese Ambivalenz drückt sich auch dadurch aus, daß meist beide denkbaren Alternativen innerhalb des Märenkorpus' als je eigene Lösung gestaltet sind. 2. Als erzählerische Grundhaltung schlägt immer wieder die Betonung des für den damaligen Leser Interessanten oder Neuen durch. Das bedeutet einmal, daß die Märenautoren nicht an der Aufstellung einer neuen Verhaltensnorm interessiert waren, sondern sie lieber die offene Situation in ihrer Ambivalenz reflektieren wollten. Neue Möglichkeiten sollten sondiert und durchgespielt werden. Die andere Beobachtung führt zu dem Schluß, daß das ungewohnte Bild der aktiven, listigen, oft sogar überlegenen Frau in ihrem ungewohnten Kontext durchaus auch als Provokation und Denkanstoß gedacht war. Auch wenn die konkrete historische Situation ein solches Verhalten noch nicht als realisierbar ansah, konnte es zumindest die Richtung als wünschenswert vorstellen. Hier spielen gewiß auch utopische Zielvorstellungen eine Rolle. Bezieht man die Textüberlieferung in die Analyse mit ein, so verstärkt sich dieser Eindruck noch dadurch, daß vom selben Motiv unterschiedliche Gestaltungen vorliegen, in denen die neue Rollentypik der Frau in ihren emanzipatorischen Tendenzen in der zeitlich späteren Version verglichen mit der ersten Textfassung mehrfach verdeutlicht oder schärfer begründet wird.

Um zusammenfassend schließlich die Frage nach der politischen Funktion der Textgattung Märe zu beantworten, ist auf die eingangs erwähnte Feststellung von Erich Köhler zurückzukommen, daß eine neue Textgattung neue Freiräume für Fragestellungen und Reflexionen eröffnet. Vor dem Hintergrund der hier kaum angedeuteten sozialhistorischen Veränderungen für die Position des Mannes und der Frau in der spätmittelalterlichen Gesellschaft bearbeitet hier eine neue Textsorte ein Problem, das in zweifacher Hinsicht aktuell ist. Zum einen sind es die veränderten historischen Ausgangspositionen selbst, die die Gesellschaft umstrukturieren. Dieser Umschichtungsprozeß will reflektiert sein. Zum andern aber, und das betrifft den Literaturwissenschaftler primär, zeigt sich, daß die tradierten literarischen Gattungen wie vor allem der Minnesang und der höfische Roman eine Idealtypik entwickeln, die sehr einseitig erscheint. Widerstände dagegen zeigen sich einerseits in der Minnetheorie etwa eines Andreas Capellanus[52] im 12. Jh., die in ihrer Kritik im nächsten Jahrhundert aber nicht durchhält, zum andern in der Gestaltung des Tristanstoffs,[53] die von den Gottfried-Fortsetzern am Ende des 13. Jahrhunderts von der explosiven Ehebruchspannung Gottfrieds von Straßburg wieder zum harmonisierenden gemeinsamen Liebestod zurückgebogen wird. Hier liegt die innerliterarische Auseinandersetzung der Märengattung, die erstmals seit dem beginnenden 13. Jh. den ganzen Fragehorizont der anthropologischen Verhaltensambivalenzen aufrollt.[54]

---

52 R. Schnell, Andreas Capellanus. Zur Rezeption des römischen und kanonischen Rechts in "De Amore". München 1982 (Münstersche Mittelalter-Schriften, 46); A. Karnein, "De Amore" in volkssprachlicher Literatur. Untersuchungen zur Andreas Capellanus-Rezeption in Mittelalter und Renaissance. Heidelberg 1985 (Beihefte z. Germ.-Roman-Monstsschrift, Bd. 4); ders., Europäische Minnedidaktik. in: Neues Handbuch d. Literaturwissenschaft, Bd. 7, hg. v. H. Kraus, Wiesbaden 1981, S. 121-144.

53 G. Weber – W. Hoffmann, Der Tristanstoff in der mittelalterlichen Dichtung. in: Weber – Hoffmann, Gottfried von Straßburg. Stuttgart 51981, Kap. III [S. 28-49] (Sammlung Metzler, M 15); F. Ranke, Tristan und Isold. München 1925 (Bücher des Mittelalters).

54 Hier wäre die richtig gestellte Frage von Monika Jonas nach dem "Textkontext" (wie Anm. 5; S. 242ff.) – es geht dabei um den Methodenansatz der 'Intertextualität' – die sie leider nicht weiter verfolgt, aufzugreifen und als vordringliches literarhistorisches Desiderat

Was Per Nykrog für die französischen Fabliaux vor Jahrzehnten schon bahnbrechend ausgeführt hat,[55] hat die germanistische Forschung bezüglich der Funktion der literarischen Form der Märengestaltung in einigen Teilen erst zögerlich begonnen. So wünschte man sich etwa eine ausführliche Behandlung der Perspektive des Humors, der Ironie und der Parodie,[56] die manche Doppelbödigkeit des Bezugshorizonts erst verdeutlichen könnte. Doch überlassen wir uns bis dahin auch gern dem naiven Charme der Mären als "contes à rire".

---

genauer zu untersuchen.

[55] Les Fabliaux. Etude d'histoire littéraire et de stylistique médiévale. Kopenhagen 1957.

[56] Karl-Heinz Schirmer hat in seinen "Stil- und Motivuntersuchungen zur mittelhochdeutschen Versnovelle" (Tübingen 1969, S. 237-298) zwar ein schönes Kapitel über die Parodie in den Schwänken vorgelegt. Doch müßte man diese Frage von der Komik bis zur Satire hin vielleicht doch noch einmal umfassender angehen. Ansätze zur schwankspezifischen Komik auch bei M. Jonas, Der spätmittelalterliche Versschwank (wie Anm. 5), S. 193-201.

Le couple impossible: Littérature et corps de la femme en Italie (de la *Vita nuova* aux "Livres de famille")

Par RAUL MORDENTI, *Università di Roma "La Sapienza"*

> "La nature de l'Autre était contraire au mélange: pour le joindre harmonieusement à l'Identique le Démiurge usa la coercition." (Platone, *Timeo*, 35a)

1. Ce discours ne peut que partir de l'observation d'une absence, de la remarque d'un *manque*: le mot "couple", dans le sens que nous lui avons donné, en effet n'existe pratiquement pas dans la littérature italienne avant Boccace.

Les dictionnaires historiques de la langue italienne[1] nous donnent deux sens différents pour le mot "*coppia*": d'un côté celui de "paire", deux éléments unis d'une manière stable et/ou logique (de là aussi l'usage du mot "couple" pour indiquer la laisse double qui attachait deux chiens); de l'autre celui dérivé du latin *copula*, lié donc au sens d'"union sexuelle", *coitus*.

Le mot se trouve déjà avec le premier sens, celui de "paire", dans *L'Esopo volgare*, où l'on parle du "couple de coups de pieds" d'un cheval; Frà Giordano da Pisa (1260-1311), dans le premier et plus important recueil de sermons conservé en langue vulgaire italienne (707 sermons conservés dans des *reportationes*), emploie "couple" pour indiquer un "couple (une paire) d'oeufs", et, toujours avec le même sens, pour rappeler que notre Créateur nous a fourni des "couples" d'organes (deux yeux, deux lèvres, deux oreilles) pour que leur usage soit plus prudent.[2]

Dans le deuxième sens le mot est utilisé par le "fou" Jacopone da Todi (1236-1306), qui oscille toujours entre mystique et excès verbal:

---

[1] Cf.: *Vocabolario degli Accademici della Crusca*, Firenze, Cellini, 1863 (5 ed.); N. Tommaseo – B. Bellini, *Dizionario della lingua italiana*, 7 voll., Torino 1861-79; S. Battaglia, *Grande Dizionario della Lingua Italiana*, Torino, Utet, 1961- .

[2] Cf.: *Prediche inedite del Beato Giordano da Rivalto dell'ordine di predicatori recitate in Firenze dal 1302 al 1305*, a cura di Enrico Narducci, Bologna, 1867; *Giordano da Pisa. Quaresimale Fiorentino 1305-1306*, edizione per cura di Carlo Delcorno, Firenze, Sansoni, 1974; *Le corps et la chair dans les sermons de Giordano da Pisa: essai d'analyse informatique*, 2 voll., Mémoire de licence présenté par Cristina Bianchi et dirigé par le Prof. Agostino Paravicini-Bagliani (Université de Lausanne, Faculté des Lettres, mars 1987).

lo quinto amore menarne ad esser desponsata
al suo figlio dolcissimo essere copulata (45, 24).

D'une façon plus appropriée, le verbe "copulare" est employé (deux fois) par le
chroniqueur florentin Matteo Villani (1280 environ-1363), mais en l'opposant
toujours au concept de mariage:

> Pour le manque de respect qu'ils eurent pour le sacrement du mariage,
> ayant *copulé* avant d'en avoir la permission... (7, 24)
> Avec laquelle il *copula* avec une telle concupiscence charnelle déréglée,
> qu'il faisait plusieurs choses débauchées et vicieuses; et il ne voulait même
> pas voir sa légitime épouse... (4, 18)[3]

Le mot "couple" n'apparaît pas chez Dante, ni dans *La vita nuova*, ni dans le
Convivio, ni dans *La divina commedia*, où l'on peut lire uniquement (dans
l'Inferno, XXIII, v. 8) le verbe "s'accoppia" par référence à la fable pseudo-
ésopique du rat et de la grenouille, que rappelle à Dante la scène des diables
Alichino et Calcabrina pris dans la poix.[4]

Mais ces différentes occurrences ne contiennent pas le puissant noyau
sémantique que nous donnons au mot "couple" aujourd'hui et qui réside justement dans la *coexistence* et dans la connection à l'intérieur du même mot, des
deux concepts: a) celui de "copulation", amour charnel, et b) celui de "paire",
de lien stable; le deux concepts référant à un homme et à une femme; en
somme "couple" pour nous aujourd'hui signifie un homme et une femme unis
par un lien (qui constituent une "paire" fixe) et qui ont des relations sexuelles
entre eux (qui "copulent" ensemble); c'est la définition que donne aussi le
récent *Vocabolario della lingua italiana*:

---

3   Cf.: *Croniche storiche di Giovanni, Matteo e Filippo Villani, a miglior lezione ridotte
     coll'aiuto dei testi a penna...*, Milano, Borroni e Scotti, 1848. Notre traduction de: "Per
     l'irriverenza ch'ebbono al sagramento matrimoniale di *copularsi* prima ch'avessono la
     dispensagione..."; "Con la quale *si copulò* con tanta e disordinata concupiscenza carnale,
     che molte dissolute e sconce cose ne faceva; e la legittima moglie non volea vedere...".

4   Volt'era in su la favola d'Isopo
     lo mio pensier per la presente rissa,
     dov'el parlò della rana e del topo;
     chè più non si pareggia "mo" e, "issa"
     che l'un con l'altro fa, se ben *s'accoppia*
     principio e fine con la mente fissa. (*If.*, XXIII, vv. 4-9).

Deux individus (…) de la même espèce, unis ou considerés ensemble (…), se référant par antonomase au couple des époux et à la vie matrimoniale, mais aussi, généralement, au couple homme-femme vivants librement ensemble.

Cette définition est encore plus évidente dans le diminutif "petit couple" (*coppietta*): "Couple d'amoureux ou de fiancés."[5]

Le mot "couple", au sens moderne que lui nous donnons, fait son apparition dans le *Decameron* I,5, dans la nouvelle de la marquise de Monferrato et de son badinage "sage et mesuré" avec le roi de France (et le fait de situer le récit dans le milieu courtois et chevaleresque de la cour de Philippe Auguste le Borgne n'est pas casuel):

il fut raporté par un Chevalier qui cognoissoit ledit Marquis, qu' en tout le monde n'y avoit un semblable *couple* en mariage que du Marquis et sa femme….[6]

Et toujours au sens moderne que nous venons de définir, le mot "couple" apparait dans les *Trionfi* de Pétrarque, et plus précisément dans le premier, le *Triumphus cupidinis*,[7] en référence à deux amoureux tragiques, Massinissa et Sofonisba:

Or dimmi, se colui in pace vi guide,
– e mostrai 'l duca lor – che *coppia* è questa
che mi par delle cose rare e fide? (2, 25-27).

2. Mais pourquoi ce mot (et le concept qui s'y rattache) n'existe-t-il pas dans la littérature pre-décaméronienne? Et sourtout pourquoi n'apparaît-il pas en Dante? On ne peut absolument pas éluder cette question, même si l'on évoque l'étendue de la production dantesque qui rend encore plus significative l'absence d'un mot. Le fait est qu'avec Dante (comme on le sait) naît à la fois (à son plus haut niveau) la littérature italienne en langue vulgaire, et la poésie qui

---

5   *Vocabolario della lingua italiana*, Roma, Istituto della Enciclopedia Italiana, 1986- , vol. I, p. 945.

6   *Le Decameron de M. Jean Bocace florentin traduit d'italien en François par M. Antoine le Maçon*, Rouen, Claude le Vilain, 1603, p. 33.

7   F. Petrarca, *Trionfi*, dans *Rime, Trionfi e poesie latine*, par F. Neri – G. Martellotti – E. Bianchi – N. Sapegno, Milano-Napoli, Ricciardi, 1951, pp. 479-578 (488).

s'interroge sur le *moi* individuel, qui affirme ouvertement les thèmes de
l'individualité du poète, et donc, au moins dans une certaine mesure, de l'autobiographie. Ces transformations s'effectuent autour d'un fort noyau thématique
irremplaçable, hérité chez Dante de la tradition courtoise et du stilnovisme: le
thème, justement, de la femme; dans le cas de Dante, l'objet et l'occasion de la
poésie c'est la femme; cette femme que le poète appelle la *sienne*, celle que,
individuellement, il a aimée et qu'il se rappelle avoir aimée.

En ce sens il est possible d'affirmer que la littérature italienne débute en parlant des femmes, en parlant "à travers les femmes" (Zancan); [8] le poète, en effet, parle de lui-même (et il élabore un nouveau moi-même) en parlant de/à
une femme.

Poésie en langue vulgaire, poésie amoureuse et poésie autobiographique de
la mémoire, découlent donc *d'une même source*, et les modalités de cette naissance ont une incomparable portée, non seulement pour la littérature italienne
mais aussi, oserais-je affirmer, pour l'*episthémé* européenne et occidentale.

C'est de ce lien indissociable entre l'*amour* pour la femme, l'*individualité*
psycologico-personnelle du poète et sa décision de *se souvenir* que naît, comme
on le sait, la *Vita nuova*:

Au débout de la *Vita nuova*, Dante écrit:

> En cette partie du livre de ma mémoire, avant laquelle il y aurait peu de
> chose à lire se trouve une rubrique qui dit: *Incipit vita nova*.
>
> Et sous cette rubrique je trouve écrites les paroles que j'ai l'intention de
> reproduire [assemplare] en ce petit livre... (I, 1). [9]

Et, plus loin, pour expliquer la naissance de la poésie en langue vulgaire,
Dante écrit:

> Et on ne compte pas un très grand nombre d'années, depuis qu'apparurent
> pour la première fois ces poètes vulgaires(...). Et le premier qui commença
> à écrire comme poète vulgaire s'y décida parce qu'il voulut faire entendre
> ses paroles à une dame, à qui il n'était guère aisé d'entendre les vers latins.
> (XXV, 4-6). [10]

---

8   "... i testi letterari, nella loro quasi totalità, parlano, sia pure in modi diversi, di donne, o
    meglio *attraverso* figure femminili." (M. Zancan, *La donne*, dans *Letteratura italiana*,
    sous la direction de A. Asor Rosa, vol. V, *Le Questioni*, Torino, Einaudi, 1986, pp. 765-
    827, 768).

9   Dante Alighieri, *Vita Nova*, traduction nouvelle par André Pézard, Paris, Nagel, 1953, p.
    69.

Mais dans son histoire amoureuse même la poésie se transforme (et Dante en est parfaitement conscient): de moyen elle devient but; de moyen pour parler à la femme et en obtenir l'amour, elle devient *le plaisir faire de la poésie* qui remplace ainsi le plaisir normalement lié à l'amour. De fait, aux femmes qui lui demandent, moqueuses, où est son plaisir, puisqu'il aime Béatrice au point de ne pouvoir supporter sa présence ("Nous te prions de nous dire où réside pour toi cette béatitude"), Dante répond:

"En ces *paroles* qui louent ma dame." (XVIII, 6).[11]

Après quoi, réfléchissant sur cette réponse, il conclut:

"Puisqu'il y a tant de béatitude dans *ces paroles* qui louent ma dame, pourquoi est-ce autrement que j'ai parlé?" (XVIII, 8).[12]

C'est de là que prend naissance la nouvelle poétique, c'est là le vrai *début* dont (une fois de plus) Dante est parfaitement conscient, au point qu'il paraît presque s'arrêter et hésiter:

Aussi je décidai de prendre pour matière de mes vers désormais ce qui serait à la louange de cette très gentille (...) et ainsi demeurais-je quelques jours avec le désir d'écrire et la peur de commencer. (XVIII, 9).[13]

La poésie, en tant que poésie d'amour, se libère ainsi de tout but référentiel, elle est *fin en elle*, elle est finalement *littérature*; de plus, elle participe (presque par transfert et métonymie) de l'érotisme qui l'a fondée et du plaisir qui lui est attaché; donc, désormais (pour la première fois et pour toujours) la poésie est "plaisir du texte", est la "béatitude" – pour parler avec Dante – qui consiste en ses propres paroles.

3. Si telle est la fonction centrale, et même fondamentale, du rapport avec la femme, il serait permis de s'attendre une présence significative d'une *relation de couple*, d'un "moi et toi" dans la *Vita nuova*.

Mais voir la *Vita nuova* comme l'histoire d'une *relation à deux*, entre Dante et Béatrice serait le résultat d'une lecture superficielle, scolaire et incorrecte. C'est plutôt *exactement le contraire*: le "petit livre" ne parle d'autre chose que de *l'impossibilité* d'une telle relation, et la poésie naît du désir continuel (presque obsédant) de dresser un *écran*, de parler *indirectement*, de s'adresser

10 *Ibidem*, p. 133.
11 *Ibidem*, p. 104.
12 *Ibidem*, pp. 104-105.
13 *Ibidem*, p. 105.

à un *troisième* interlocuteur pour que le deuxième puisse le recevoir, en fin d'un *triangle érotique* (ou mieux: *une triangulation de la communication amoureuse*), un triangle érotique vraiment paradoxal, puisqu'il vit de la chasteté, et qu'il sera intéressant de confronter avec celui qu'a remarquablement étudié Michel Olsen.[14]

Comment s'établit ce "triangle" dans la *Vita nuova*?

Alors que Dante est en train de regarder Béatrice, son regard est intercepté par hasard par une autre femme (la "femme-écran") qui se trouve sur la ligne idéale de ses yeux:

"... se trouvait à mi-chemin sur la ligne droite qui partait de la trés-gentille Béatrice et se terminait à mes yeux" (*VN*, V, 2).[15]

Le triangle de la communication amoureuse consiste donc dans les trois éléments Béatrice-femme/écran-yeux de Dante.

S'étant aperçu que ce regard intercepté fait naître chez ceux qui l'entourent la conviction que son amour s'adresse à cette seconde femme, et non à Béatrice, Dante entretient l'equivoque qui lui permet d'aimer plus librement Béatrice et de lui adresser des poésies d'amour sans crainte de l'offenser; de cette manière Dante transforme l'élément "femme/écran", qui intercepte la communication des regards, en élément qui consent à la communication de la poésie, puisque cette femme lui permet d'adresser des poésies à Béatrice en feignant de parler à la femme/ écran. Le triangle s'établit alors, intentionnellement, s u r les trois sommets Dante-femme/écran-Béatrice.

Pour consolider cet équivoque, et le rendre plus vraisemblable aux yeux du public (qui représente donc un "troisième terme" constant et structurel dans l'histoire d'amour de la *Vita nuova*) Dante va jusqu'à composer quelques poésies dédiées à la femme/écran pour faire croire que son amour s'adresse à elle:

"et pour en faire plus accroire aux gens, je fis pour elle quelques petites choses en vers" (V, 4).[16]

Il faut remarquer que la poésie écrite par Dante pour la femme/écran est un "sonnet rinterziato", sur le model de Guittone, dit aussi "double", c'est à dire ayant un vers de sept pieds ajouté après le premier et le troisième vers de chaque quartine et après le deuxième de chaque tercet, rimant avec le vers

---

[14] Cf.: M. Olsen, *Les Transformations du Triangle Erotique*, København, Akademisk Forlag, 1976; Id., *Amore e virtù nella novellistica rinascimentale. Argomentazione narrativa e ricezione letteraria*, Napoli, Federico & Ardia, 1984.

[15] D. Alighieri, *Vita Nova*, *cit*., p. 76.

[16] *Ibidem*.

précédent (selon le schéma: AaBAaB AaBAaB CDdC DCcD), et que le sonnet est "double" également du point de vue sémantique, et non seulement métrique, à commencer par le début, qui rappelle presque littéralement la lamentation de Géremia (*Lam 1.12: "O vos omnes qui transitis per vias atendite et videte si est dolor sicut dolor meus"*).

> O voi che per la via d'Amor passate,
> attendete e guardate
> s'elli è dolore alcun, quanto 'l mio, grave (VII, 3).
> (O vous qui passez par le chemin d'Amour
> prêtez-moi attention, et voyez
> s'il est une douleur aussi lourde que la mienne.)

Ainsi, une poésie d'amour est placée sous l'enseigne, tout à fait trompeuse, d'un texte biblico-religieux, jusqu'à la conclusion:

> Sì che volendo far come coloro
> che per vergogna celan lor mancanza
> di fuor mostro allegranza,
> e dentro de lo core struggo e ploro (VII, 6).
> (Aussi, voulant faire comme ceux
> qui par honte cachent leur faiblesse,
> au dehors je fais montre d'allégresse
> et au fond de mon coeur je me consume et pleure.)[17]

Conclusion qui est le triomphe de la duplicité, de l'oxymore, de la coexistence contracdictoire des oppositions, entièrement construite sur la simulation et sur une série de couples antithétiques: dehors/dedans, les autres/fond de mon coeur, montrer/être, allégresse/je me consume et je pleure.

Ce jeu d'écrans est tellement contraignant pour Dante que, lorsque la première femme/écran quitte Florence, il doit la remplacer (par conseil de l'Amour qui lui est apparu en rêve) par une *seconde* femme/écran:
"qui sera *la défense* comme l'était celle-ci" (IX, 5-6).[18]

Le triangle prend alors une nouvelle configuration: Dante-deuxième femme/écran-Béatrice.

Et de même quand Amour lui commande de parler à Béatrice, Dante est-il obligé de recourir à l'écran qui représente cette fois la ballade elle-même:

---

17   *Ibidem*, p. 78.

18   *Ibidem*, p. 82.

"Ces vers, fais qu'ils soient comme un intermédiaire, de façon que *tu ne parles pas directement à elle*, ce qui 'est pas convenable..." (XII, 8). [19]

Également, dans la *Ballata, i' voi*, Dante prie cette même ballade pour qu'elle retrouve Amour et que tous deux aillent "au devant de ma dame" (donc: Dante-Ballade-Béatrice). Il s'agit dans ce cas d'un triangle pour ainsi dire, "impropre", et Dante lui-même s'interroge à ce propos, en se demandant si la ballade peut être considérée à bon droit comme un "troisième élément", puisqu'elle consiste dans les mots mêmes du poète:

> On pourrait sans doute me faire une objection, et dire que l'on ne sait guère à qui peut s'adresser mon discours à la seconde personne, parce que la ballade n'est pas autre chose que les paroles mêmes que je prononce. (XII, 7). [20]

Ici, une fois encore, la conscience qu'a Dante des modalités de son propre discours, est remarquable, comme est remarquable, toutefois, la force de l'interdiction de s'adresser directement à Béatrice.

C'est pourquoi Dante se propose d'écrire

> ...des vers, dans lesquels, m'adressant à elle, j'expliquerais ce qui me faisait changer de figure, et dirais que *je sais bien* que cette cause *reste ignorée*, et que *si on la savait*, on prendrait, je *crois* mon sort en pitié; et je resolus de les écrire avec le désir qu'ils pussent un jour arriver à ses oreilles. (XIV, 10). [21]

Et l'une des plus belles chansons d'amour de la littérature italienne (et pas uniquement italienne), c'est introduite encore de nouveau par la déclaration de l'impossibilité de parler à Béatrice (et de Béatrice) sans l'écran, (dans ce cas l'écran des autres femmes, donc selon le triangle Dante-femmes-Béatrice):

> ... il me vint un tel désir de faire de vers, que je commençai à envisager la voie que je devrais prendre; et je pensai que *parler d'elle n'était pas convenable de ma part que si je m'adressais à des dames à la seconde personne* (...)
> Donne ch'avete intelletto d'amore,

---

[19] *Ibidem*, p. 90.

[20] *Ibidem*, p. 88.

[21] *Ibidem*, p. 96.

i' vo' con voi de la mia donna dire... (XIX, 1-4).
(Dames qui avez intelligence d'amour,
c'est avec vous que je veux parler de ma dame...).[22]

Encore: après la mort de Béatrice un de ses parents (Manetto Portinari?)
s'adresse à Dante pour lui demander:

"... de lui écrire des vers pour une dame qui était morte; et il *déguisait* ses
paroles, de façon à avoir l'air de parler d'une autre..." (XXXII, 2).[23]

(Donc, dans ce cas, le triangle est double: Manetto-femme morte/écran-Béatrice;
et ensuit: Dante-femme morte/écran-Béatrice).

Il est dans tout cas certain que cette interdiction de parler de façon directe à
la femme aimée est un formidable *générateur de poésie*: cette triangulation
obligée de l'expression amoureuse ouvre un gigantesque espace poétique que
la tradition (il suffit de nommer Pétrarque) approfondira et explorera dans
toutes les diréctions; le refus du discours direct et référentiel entraîne (et
permet) un état d'âme confus, et instaure le règne (poétique par excellence) de
la périphrase, de l'exagération, de la variété, de l'incertitude, de la métaphore,
de l'oxymore:

Tutti li miei penser parlan d'Amore;
e hanno in lor sì gran *varietate*,
ch'*altro* mi fa voler sua potestade,
altro folle ragiona il suo valore,
altro sperando m'apporta dolzore,
altro pianger mi fa spesse fiate;
(...)
Ond'*io non so* da qual matera prenda;
e *vorrei dire*, e *non so ch'io mi dica*:
così mi trovo in amorosa *erranza*!
E se con tutti voi fare accordanza,
convenemi chiamar la mia *nemica*,
madonna la Pietà, *che mi difenda* (XIII, 8-9).
(Tous mes pensers parlent d'Amour;
et ils sont entre eux si grandement *divers*
que *l'un* me fait souhaiter son empire,

---

[22] *Ibidem*, pp. 105-106.
[23] *Ibidem*, pp. 149-150.

> *l'autre* me dit qu'il est fou de lui donner pouvoir sur nous;
> un *autre*, quand j'espère m'apporte douceur,
> un *autre* me fait pleurer maintes fois;
> (...)
> Aussi *je ne sais* duquel tirer matière,
> et *je voudrais parler* et *je ne sais que dire*:
> à tel point je me trouve égaré dans les tourments amoureux.
> Et si je veux faire accord entre tous
> il me faut appeler mon *ennemie*,
> madame la Pitié, pour *qu'elle me défende*).[24]

C'est la dialectique entre l'être et le paraître, entre le vouloir et le non vouloir, c'est *l'odi et amo* de Catulle qui du point de vue strictement sémiotique, est consenti, justement et uniquement, par ce *langage indirect*, oblique, masqué.

4. Pour revenir à notre sujet, on peut à juste titre affirmer que chez l'Auteur (et dans le texte) exemplaire de notre littérature d'amour, est catégoriquement exclue avant tout pour des raisons sémiotiques, toute possibilité d'un rapport direct "à deux", de *couple*, au moment même où est crée le modèle littéraire de l'*amour* (modèle qui, comme on le sait, durera longtemps, très longtemps).

D'où vient cette contradiction, et plus encore, cette *incompatibilité*, entre les deux concepts de "couple" et d'"amour" et entre les deux champs sémantiques respectifs?

Dans le *Trattato d'amore*[25] de Andrea Cappellano (1196 environ), on trouve, en même temps que la définition rigoureuse (et la plus célèbre) de l'amour au Moyen Age, les fondements théoriques de cette incompatibilité.

Avant tout (dans le premier chapitre de son *Trattato*) voyons la définition que donne Cappellano:

> L'Amour est une passion innée, générée au-dehors de la pensée, par laquelle on ressent le désir effréné d'embrasser une autre personne et d'accomplir avec elle tout ce qui est commandé par l'Amour. [26]

---

[24] *Ibidem*, pp. 93-94.

[25] Cf. A. Cappellano, *Trattato d'amore (De amore libri tres)*, par S. Battaglia, Roma, Perrella, 1947.

[26] "Amor est passio quaedam innata procedens ex visione et immoderata cogitatione formae alterius sexus, ob quam aliquis super omnia cupit alterius potiri amplexibus et omnia de utriusque voluntate in ipsius amplexu amoris praecepta compleri." (A. Cappellano, *op,*

Il ne s'agit donc pas (et il faut le souligner) de l'innocent amour platonique dont parle Cappellano; tant il est vrai qu'il se hâte de décrire "les quatre degrés de l'amour"; avoir et donner l'espoir d'amour; embrasser; "se serrer plusieurs fois dans les bras"; "secret abandon de toute sa personne"; et il précise en outre que si l'on désire commencer par le premier degré il est préférable de se confier à quelq'un qui ne soit pas experimenté, et au contraire que si l'on désire commencer par le quatrième degré il vaut mieux se confier à une personne déjà expérimentée.[27]

Mais, si l'amour dont nous parle Cappellano n'est pas platonique, il n'est pas non plus conjugal; au contraire! (et ne cesse toujours de nous surprendre, au cours des siècles, sa nette affirmation à propos de l'*incompatibilité* entre amour et relation matrimoniale de couple):

> Il est pour moi très étonnant que puisse exister le désir d'amour entre ceux qui sont unis par le mariage! Ils veulent ravir le mot d'amour! Il est évident que l'amour ne peut pas trouver sa place dans le mariage (…) Il est désormais clair qu'entre vous et votre mari il ne peut pas y avoir d'amour.[28]

Et c'est cette impossibilité même d'aimer dans le mariage qui, avec le droit-devoir naturel d'aimer, fait paradoxalement de l'adultère non seulement un acte permis, mais justifié pour la femme "honnête".

> Ainsi, pour chaque femme honnête il est bien d'aimer sagement, et sans offenser votre mari vous pouvez accepter mes prières et me donner votre amour.[29]

D'ailleurs, insiste Cappellano, non sans une malicieuse cohérence théologique, une fois établi que l'amour sexuel qui n'a pas pour finalité la procréation est de toute façon défendu, et qu'il est même plus grave de "mal utiliser" une "bonne chose" comme le mariage, il en résulte que si existait un grand amour

---

cit., p. 4).

[27] *Ibidem*, p. 39.

[28] "Vehementer tamen admiror, quod maritalem affectionem quidem, quam quilibet inter se coniugati adinvicem post matrimonii copulam tenentur habere; vos vultis amoris sibi vocabulum usurpare, quum liquide constet inter virum et uxorem amorem sibi locum vindicare non posset. (…) Unde liquide vobis constat, inter vos et virum vestrum amorem nullatenus posse vigere." (*Ibidem*, p. 166, 168).

[29] "Ergo, quum cuilibet probae expediat mulieri prudenter, amare, sine vestra igitur iniuria potestis petentis preces admittere et vestro postulantem amore ditare." (*Ibidem*, p. 168).

entre deux époux il pourrait être considéré comme le plus grave des adultères:

"Il est plus grave de forniquer avec sa femme qu'avec une autre femme. Un amoureux fou de son épouse est le pire des adultères, selon l'apôtre."[30]

Ailleurs, Cappellano fait la distinction entre "dilectio" (qui existe entre parents, par exemple entre père et fils, et l'on présume aussi entre époux) et "amicitia" (qui ne peut exister qu'entre libres amants).

La conclusion du différend entre celui qui soutient ces positions et la femme qui refuse l'amour est laissée, dans le *Trattato*, à la comtesse Marie de Champagne elle-même, qui intervient pour mettre fin au débat avec une lettre, non exempte d'une solennité signigicative.

Il ne faut pas sousestimer l'importance de la forme choisie par Cappellano pour organiser et exprimer ce message particulier: l'oeuvre consiste de fait en une série de dialogues imaginaires (et exemplaires) entre les amants, selon la combinatoire de leurs différents nivaux sociaux ("Comment l'homme bien né doit parler à la femme du peuple", "Comment l'homme bien né doit parler à la femme bien née", et ainsi de suite jusqu'à "Comment celui de haute naissance doit parler à la femme de haute naissance"), tandis que deux chapitres ultérieurs sont dédiés à l'amour de moines et de soeurs (ce dernier réprouvé avec extrême véhémence et sévérité) et à d'autres questions secondaires.

Dans aucun autre passage la conclusion n'est soustraite aux interlocuteurs imaginaires et confiée à une figure extradiégétique; dans ce cas, qui parle est la plus remarquable figure du milieu dans lequel naquit l'oeuvre (la comtesse elle-même qui parle à la première personne). Il serait donc difficile de considérer comme peu importante, ou toute plaisante, la sentence prononcée par la comtesse. La voici:

Affirmons et soutenons que l'amour ne peut pas étendre sa juridiction jusqu' aux deux époux. Car les amants accordent tout l'un à l'autre sans aucune nécessité extérieure, tandis que les époux sont obligés d'obéir l'un à l'autre, et ils ne peuvent rien se nier l'un à l'autre.[31]

Les arguments de la comtesse de Champagne se développent avec cohérence:

---

30 "Nam vehemens amator, ut apostolica lege docetur, in propria uxore iudicatur adulter." (*Ibidem*, p. 172.

31 "Dicimus enim et stabilito tenore firmamus, amorem non posse suas inter duos iugales extendere vires. Nam amantes sibi invicem gratis omnia largiuntur nullius necessitatis ratione cogente. Iugales vero mutuis tenentur ex debito voluntatibus obedire et in se nullo se ipsos sibi invicem denegare." (*Ibidem*, p. 180).

aimer son époux n'est pas honorable, parce que sa personne nous appartient déjà, entre le mari et la femme ne peut exister la jalousie, sans laquelle il n'y a pas de véritable amour, etc.

5. Une deuxième pièce, différente mais symétrique et qui s'assemble parfaitement avec la première, vient s'ajouter à notre mosaïque: si Dante, dans *la Vita nuova* nous démontre l'impossibilité d'une relation de couple (un "moi-toi") dans la communication amoureuse, Cappellano nous donne les bases éthiques et anthropologiques d'une telle impossibilité; l'amour conçu comme valeur inconciliable avec le mariage, et plus encore fondé sur l'opposition absolue et de principe avec le mariage. La littérature, et la littérature d'amour en particulier, trace ainsi au cours du Moyen Age une frontière rigoureuse et durable; mais, comme il arrive toujours, une frontière suppose surtout un ennemi, la construction d'un mur parle avant tout de la présence d'un "autre", c'est à dire de la nécessité d'une *exclusion*.

Il faut donc se demander: qu'est-ce qui reste exclu du cercle lumineux de la littérature d'amour? Quelle realité est frappée de l'interdiction d'être prononcée et de se prononcer?

Les mouvements politiques des femmes et les études qui en dérivent, nous permettent de hasarder une réponse à cette question qui, avant eux, n'était pas même formulable: ce qui *reste au dehors*, l'"autre" irréductible qui a contraint l'amour occidental à s'organiser selon le bizarre statut de l'amour courtois, est en réalité *une "autre"*, c'est la femme, et, plus particulièrement, son corps.

Encore une fois il est possible de lire la *Vita nuova* comme l'allégorie exemplaire et fondamentale de l'amour littéraire: Béatrice apparaît sous forme d'un corps inquiétant *au début* de l'histoire d'amour; elle est nue, à peine couverte d'un léger voile rouge sang, endormie entre les bras d'Amour; puis elle mange le coeur de poète; c'est la vision-rêve tout de suite après la fatale deuxième rencontre à dix-huit ans, et la naissance de l'amour:

Dans ses bras [d'Amour] il me semblait voir dormir une personne nue, sauf qu'elle me paressait enveloppée légèrement dans une etoffe de soie couleur de sang. Et en la regardant avec une grande attention, je reconnus que c'était la dame du salut ... (III, 4).[32]

Une pareille vision c'est tout à fait inconcevable *au terme* du parcours ascétique

---

[32] D. Alighieri, *Vita Nova*, cit., p. 73.

que le livre (et la vie même de Dante) décrit, et plus encore, on peut dire que le "petit livre" lui-même ne sert pas à autre chose qu'à rendre impossible une telle vision, à la dépasser, à la sublimer.

Mais remontons encore dans le temps, avant Dante et Andrea, jusqu'au mythe fondamental et archetypique de l'*amour fou* (mais aussi de l'amour malheureux et défendu, de l'amour incroyable et impossible), c'est à dire à Abélard et Héloïse et à leur inconcevable correspondance, texte tellement en contradiction avec les règles établies et transmises qu'il continue à alimenter les discussions (pas uniquement philologiques) sur son sens, et jusqu'à sa crédibilité, sa paternité/ maternité, et même son existence.

Il y a un passage décisif dans cette correspondance; et il serait peut-être possible de lire la correspondance entière (et l'apologétique autobiographique *Historia* qui l'accompagne) comme le cadre et la préparation de ce passage capital, ce qui l'explique et le rend possible; c'est quand, dans la cinquième lettre, Abélard engage Héloïse à se résigner, et même à remercier Dieu, en s'abandonnant à une sorte d'hymne contre la condition fémminine:

> Venez-vous joindre à moi, soyez ma compagne inséparable dans l'action de grâce, puisque vous avez partagé la faute et le pardon. (…)
>
> Oh! Quel affreux malheur! Quelle perte irréparable si, réduite aux impuretés des plaisirs charnels, vous *enfantiez* avec douleur un petit nombre d'enfants pour le monde, tandis que vous engendrez avec joie une famille nombreuse pour le ciel!
>
> Vous ne seriez qu'une femme [*nec esses plus quam femina*], vous qui êtes maintenant supérieure aux hommes et qui avez échangé la malédiction d'Ève pour la benediction de Marie.
>
> Quelle profanation si ces mains sacrées qui interrogent chaque page des divines Écritures étaient condamnées aux soins vulgaires et avilissants qui sont de le partage des femmes [*curae muliebri obscenitatibus deservirent*].[33]

Dans ce but il exhorte Héloïse à *se taire*, et même, ce qui est encore plus révélateur, à ne parler que par les mots que lui-même, Abélard, a écrit pour elle, pour qu'elle les prononce comme prière.

---

[33] *Abailard et Héloïse, essai historique* par M. et M.me Guizot, *suivi des Lettres d'Abailard et d'Héloïse, traduites sur les manuscrits de la Bibliothèque Royale* par M. Oddoul…, Paris, Didier, 1853, pp. 155-156.

Afin d'assurer l'accueil que vous ferez à ma demande, et pour que rien n'en retarde l'accomplissement, je me hâte de vous envoyer la prière que *j*'ai composée pour *nos* besoins mutuels, et que *vous* réciterez humblement avec vos religeuses....[34]

Et Héloïse obéit (sixième lettre):

Il ne sera pas dit que vous pourrez une fois m'accuser de désobéissance: ma parole sera modérée, sinon ma douleur, et votre défense lui servira de frein. Je veux prendre sur moi de supprimer, *du moins en vous écrivant*, ces faiblesses contre lesquelles il est difficile, ou plutôt impossible, de se prémunir dans un entretien.(...) J'empêcherai donc ma main d'écrire, si je ne puis empêcher ma langue de parler. Plût à Dieu que mon coeur malade fût aussi disposé que ma plume à m'obéir![35]

Après le geste d'Abélard, la parole exprimée par la femme amoureuse, la parole d'Heloïse qui résonnait comme un scandale et une folie (qui ne se souvient pas du: "Quoique le nom d'épouse soit jugé plus saint et plus fort, un autre aurait toujours été plus doux à mon coeur celui de votre maîtresse, et, le dirais-je sans vous choquer, celui de votre concubine et votre fille de joie...")[36] la parole féminine écrite et même excessive et dé-réglée, la parole sexuée et physique de la femme, est bannie pour des siècles de l'horizon de notre culture; Héloïse, d'ailleurs, accepte aussitôt l'interdiction en ce qui concerne l'écriture, mais (il faut le remarquer), garde pour son amour/douleur l'espace, marginal et subalterne, de la parole prononcée, volatile, féminine justement.

6. Le long silence des femmes que consacre l'obéissance d'Héloïse, que reflètent les conseils de Cappellano, et que la poétique de Dante sanctionne pour toujours, semble, certes, définitif et irrécupérable; il existe cependant un endroit, dans l'univers textuel du bas moyen-âge, où l'on parle de *couple matrimonial*, c'est-à-dire de corps qui s'unissent dans le mariage, qui accouchent, allaitent, tombent malades, meurent; un endroit où l'on parle des femmes et du triangle fatal naissance-coït-mort.

Ces sont les livres mémoires, écrits et transmis de père en fils et destinés à

---

[34] *Ibidem*, p. 162.
[35] *Ibidem*, p. 166.
[36] *Ibidem*, p. 109.

conserver et à transmettre le patrimoine de la connaissance de la famille, que nous avons proposé d'appeler les "livres de famille".[37]

Il est possible, à partir de cet endroit impropre et liminaire, mais en même temps placé au coeur même de l'univers privé du Moyen Age (probablement dans le coffre où l'on conserve les livres des comptes), de jeter un coup d'oeil révélateur sur la réalité quotidienne du couple que la littérature transfigure et occulte?

En tous les cas, il est certain que la femme, et plus précisement son corps, ne peut pas être exclue des livres de famille, qui se bâtissent autour d'un noyau de mémoires essentiel, celui qui est justement représenté par les enregistrements des mariages, des naissances et des morts, et des dotations relatives, héritages, litiges, etc.

Le *corpus* objet de notre recherche sur les "livres de famille" en Italie, n'est pas seulement vaste et inexploré mais encore indéfini, puisque on a retrouvé des livres de famille dans presque toutes les régions italiennes et bien au delà de la période XVeme et XVIeme siècles, par exemple des livres du début de notre siècle, ou des livres écrits par des juifs romains du dix-huitième siècle, par des artisans d'Ascoli Piceno, et même par une femme de Trento.

Mais, dans notre contexte, il suffira de jeter un coup d'oeil sur le domaine plus caractéristique et traditionnel, c'est à dire les livres de mémoires écrits pour la plupart dans le milieu marchand de la Toscane entre le XIVème et le XVème siècle.

C'est dans ces milieux, justement, que se manifeste en effet clairement une conception du mariage et du couple qui assure la victoire définitive de la seculaire guerre combattue par l'église, comme écrit George Duby, "sur deux fronts":

… contre le nicolaïsme, la réticence des clercs à se déprendre des liens conjugaux, leur revendication d'user eux aussi le mariage comme d'un recours, comme un remède à la fornication (…), et contre, d'autre part,

---

[37] Cf.: R. Mordenti, *Il racconto familiare fra epica e romanzo*, dans *Narrare: percorsi possibili*, par M. di Fazio, Ravenna, Longo, 1989, pp. 135-144; A. Cicchetti – R. Mordenti, *La scrittura dei libri di famiglia*, dans *Letteratura italiana*, sous la direction de A. Asor Rosa, vol. III, *Le forme del testo*, t. 2 *La Prosa*, Torino, Einaudi, 1984, pp. 1117-1159; Idd., *I libri di famiglia in Italia*, I, *Filologia e storiografia letteraria*, Roma, Edizioni di Storia e Letteratura, 1985.

On peut lire, à propos des "livres de famille" et de "l'opposition entre deux systèmes d'écriture" en Italie, les observations de A. Petrucci, *Pouvoir de l'écriture, pouvoir sur l'écriture dans la Renaissance italienne*, dans "Annales ESC", juillet-aout 1988, n. 4, pp. 823-847 (pp. 842-844).

l'hyperascétisme, la conviction que tout commerce charnel est fornication et qui conduit à refuser radicalement le mariage (...). En conduisant enfin à son terme la construction d'une idéologie du mariage chrétien. Celle-ci repose en partie, contre le catharisme, sur la justification, la *dé-culpabilisation* de l'oeuvre de la chair.[38]

7. Quelle idée de "couple" émerge de ces textes?

Le *Libro dei buoni costumi* de Paolo da Certaldo[39] un recueil de conseils de conduite, sous forme d'aphorismes du XIV ème siècle dans un milieu marchand peut servir à expliquer cette conception de la femme et du couple: il s'agit d'une conception essentiellement eugénésique, c'est-à-dire qui met à la première place le problème de l'efficacité reproductive, de l'hérédité, de la santé, de la fécondité féminine, et qui lie à ces buts primaires les facteurs éthiques qui en découlent, comme la chastété, la fidelité, la docilité.

Paolo conseille:

Quand tu épouseras une femme, sois attentif à ce qu'elle soit née d'un bon père et d'une bonne mère, et que sa grande-mère ait joui d'une bonne réputation, parce qu'il est difficile qu'une fille née d'une bonne mère et d'une bonne grande-mère soit méchante. Fais aussi attention que la femme ne soit pas née d'une famille de malades ou de poitrinaires ou de fous, ou de teigneux ou de goutteux, parce que les enfants qui vont naître d'elle souffriront, tous ou quelques-uns de ces vices et maladies... (91).[40]

D'autre part il donne un conseil particulier sur la manière de se conduire avec sa femme pendant sa grossesse:

"... il faut beaucoup d'attention, parce qu'il y a grand risque..." (154)

---

[38] G. Duby, *Le mariage dans la société du haut Moyen Age*, dans *Il matrimonio nella società altomedievale*, Settimana di Studio del Centro Italiano di Studi sull'Alto Medioevo, XXIV, t. I, Spoleto, Presso la Sede del Centro, 1977, pp. 13-39. (32).

[39] On peut lire le *Libro* de Paolo da Certaldo, dans *Mercanti scrittori. Ricordi nella Firenze tra Medioevo e Rinascimento*, par V. Branca, Milano, Rusconi, 1986, pp. 1-99.

[40] Notre traduction de: "Quando tu pigli moglie, guarda bene ch'ella sia nata di buono padre e di buona madre, e che l'avola sia suta donna di buona fama, che rade volte fia buona la madre della fanciulla e l'avola che la fanciulla sia rea. Anche guarda molto che la moglie che pigli non sia nata da schiatta di malati o di tisichi o di gottosi, chè spesse volte avverrà che figliuoli che di lei nasceranno, sentiranno, o tutti o alcuni, d'alcuno de' detti vizi e magagne. (pp. 15-16).

Elle doit travailler peu, boire peu de vin, ne pas s'asseoir ou se coucher à terre, il faut satisfaire ses envies alimentaires;[41] il s'agit de soins plus encore remarquables parce qu'ils contredisent la brutale différence conseillée, jusque dans l'alimentation, entre les enfants de sexe masculin et feminin. Seul le fils doit étudier, tandis que la fille:

"... fais-la coudre et non lire, car il n'est pas trop convenable pour une femme de savoir lire, au cas où tu ne voudrais pas en faire une soeur...."[42]

Jusqu'à la nourriture qui est reservée aux garçons: pour les filles la quantité nécessaire pour survivre suffit; mais (et c'est éloquent) ... des vêtements meilleurs:

Le garçon fais-le bien manger et habilles-le comme tu peux (...) la fille habilles-la bien et comment tu la fais manger n'a pas d'importance, pourvu qu'elle reste vivante... (155).[43]

Aussi, la comparaison entre la femme et le cheval (qui existe dejà dans le *Decameron*, IX,9,7 et dans Sacchetti 86) ne suprendra pas trop:

"Bon cheval et mauvais cheval veulent éperon; bonne femme ou méchante femme veulent maître, et coups de bâton." (209).[44]

Et pourtant, pour Paolo da Certaldo, l'épouse doit être *aimée*, et même, (ce qui contredit totalement ce que conseille Andrea Cappellano) *seule* l'épouse doit être aimée:

"Garde-toi de tomber amoureux d'une femme qui ne soit pas ton épouse..." (135).[45]

La raison de ce conseil est surtout marchande: de toute façon, toutes les femmes sont faites de la même manière et l'une en vaut une autre (cela rappelle justement le mot de la marquise de Monferrato du *Decameron* I,5 que nous avons déjà réncontrée!); et en plus tomber amoureux en dehors du mariage est très dangereux:

---

41 *Ibidem*, p. 35.

42 Notre traduction de: "E s'ell' è fanciulla femina, polla a cuscire e none a leggere, che non istà troppo bene a una femina sapere leggere, se già no la volessi fare monaca..." (p. 36).

43 "Il fanciullo maschio pasci bene, e vesti come puoi (...) la fanciulla femina vesti bene, e come la pasci no le cale, pur ch'abbia sua vita." (p. 36).

44 "Buon cavallo e mal cavallo vuole sprone; buona donna e male donna vuol signore, e tale bastone." (p. 43).

45 "Guardati non t'innamori di femina niuna se non è tua moglie" (p. 29).

... trop grand est le danger. Parce que tous les grands déshonneurs, hontes, péchés et dépenses arrivent par les femmes; et l'on acquiert de grandes hostilités et l'on perd de grandes amitiés (135).[46]

Dans la hiérarchie des amours, que Paolo établit, la femme n'arrive qu'à la troisième place; à la première la propre âme, à la deuxième les enfants et seulement à la troisième l'amour "pour ta femme, c'est à dire, pour une bonne épouse" (à la quatrième place les amis) (156).

La réalité des couples mariés, telle qu'elle ressort des enregistrements des livres de famille, reflète sans aucun doute ce système de valeurs.

Mais une fois de plus, c'est le silence qui parle: c'est à dire qu'il arrive souvent que, dans la reconstitution au début du livre de la généalogie à l'usage de la descendance, celui qui écrit ne soit même pas capable de citer le nom des femmes de la famille, alors qu'il sait dire au contraire avec précision le montant de la dot.

Par exemple, Giovanni Morelli (XVᵉᵐᵉ siècle) parlant de son aïeul Galtieri écrit:

... Il prit pour femme je ne sais qui, mais il en eut une belle dot, d'environ cinq cents lires, et cela veut dire qu'elle était d'honorable famille.[47]

Les livres de famille confirment aussi la priorité de l'amour pour les enfants par rapport à celui pour la femme, et également c'est clair que l'on se marie dans *le but* d'avoir des enfants, des enfants mâles. A ce propos, les conseils d'"hygiène sexuelle" que note Giovanni Morelli sont très intéressants: pour avoir tout de suite des enfants, et des fils mâles, et des enfants sains, il faut avoir peu de rapports sexuels avec sa femme, jusqu'au point d'apprendre à sa femme à se lever et à s'enfuir du lit conjugal dans le cas où il risquerait d'y avoir des excès (comme il dit: de "se laisser aller"):

---

46   "... e pensa che tutte sono femine, e tutte sono fatte a uno modo: e però non porre più amore a l'una ch'a l'altra, chè troppo è grande pericolo. In però che tutti i grandi disinori, vergogne, peccati e spese s'acquistano per femine; e acquistansene il grandi nimistà, e perdonsene le grandi amistadi..." (*ibidem*).

47   Giovanni di Pagolo Morelli, *Ricordi*, dans *Mercanti scrittori, cit.*, pp. 101-339 (121): "... e' tolse moglie, non so chi fu, ma e' nebbe buona dota, circa di lire cinquecento, e questoè segno ch' ell' era d' orrevoli genti" (notre traduction): Giovanni parle de Galtieri di Calandro Morelli, mort en 1220.

... couche modérément avec elle, et ne te laisse pas aller. Et si tu veux te
conduire ainsi, il te convient de l'accoutumer à ne pas avoir trop d'habitude
avec toi; et que si elle s'apercoit que tu veux aller plus loin, qu'elle s'enfuie
et sorte du lit (...). Et il vaut mieux que tu fasses la même chose de ton
côté, que tu fuies devant la furie; reste peu chez toi, pars à la campagne,
fais un peu d'exercice, pour que cela puisse te sortir de l'esprit; (...) Et en
agissant ainsi tu auras bientôt des enfants, et ils seront bien vigoureux et forts
et grands, et ce sera des garçons, et tu resteras jeune et frais, tu demeureras
sain et gai, et tu feras toute sorte de bien. Au contraire, tu te dérègleras la
santé, tu seras malade de l'estomac et des reins, et tu détraqueras ta femme
(et toi plus encore!) et auras peu d'enfants, et des poitrinaires, des filles, des
faibles, etc.[48]

La réalité de la vie de couple qui se manifeste dans ces livres est tout à fait
impressionante: nous assistons en effet presque "en prise directe", avec l'enregistrement scrupuleux des naissances et même des avortements, à un
véritable *massacre de femmes* qui pendant des siècles a marqué notre civilisation.

Il suffit d'un seul exemple, qui n'est (remarquons-le bien) pas du tout
exceptionnel: celui de Goro (Gregorio) de Stagio Dati (1362-1435), marchand
florentin, frère d'un Leonardo Dati qui fut général des Dominicains.

Goro Dati enregistre sur son *Libro segreto*[49] ses quatre mariages, les dots,
et les filiations qui en résultent (et il n'oublie même pas un fils illégitime né
d'une esclave tartare): sa première femme, Bandecca Berardi, épousée en no-
vembre 1388, meurt des suites de fausses couches en juillet 1390; sa deuxième
femme, Isabetta, épousée en juin 1393, accouche de huit enfants, avant de
mourir d'un accouchement en juillet 1402 (donc, huit enfants en neuf ans!).
Goro Dati enregistre ainsi sa mort:

---

48   Notre traduction de: "... usa temperatamente con lei, e non ti lasciare punto trasandare. E
     se vuoi potere fare questo, ti conviene ammaestrare lei che non si dimestichi troppo teco;
     come che s'ella vede tu voglia trasandare, ella ti fugga dinanzi, eschi dal letto (...). E
     simile ti conviene fare at te, levarti dinanzi alla furia; istà poco in casa, vattene in contado,
     datti a qualche esercizio, acciò t'esca di mente; (...) E facendo questo tu arai prestamente
     figliuoli, tu gli arai bene granati e forti e grandi, tu gli arai maschi, tu ti manterrati giovane
     e fresco, tu istarai sano e allegro, tu farai ogni bene. Al contrario, ti guasterai, ti ammalerai
     stomaco e reni, rovinerai la moglie (ma più te!) avrai figli pochi, tisichi, femmine, deboli,
     etc." (*ibidem*, p. 170).

49   G. Dati, *Libro segreto*, par Carlo Gargiolli, Bologna, Romagnoli, 1869; maintenant on
     peut lire une anthologie du *Libro segreto* (selon une nouvelle édition ciritique préparée
     par Leonida Pandimiglio) dans *Mercanti scrittori...*, *cit.*, pp.547-554.

"Et alors elle alla au Paradis ma femme Isabetta (...) et c'est pourquoi je ne puis plus inscrire d'enfants d'elle. Que Dieu soit béni."

Après il tire les conclusions, exactement comme s'il s'agissait d'un compte de commerce:

"Sont nés de Betta et de moi huit enfants, c'est à dire 5 garçons et 3 filles".[50]

Même pas un an après, au mois de mai 1403, Goro se marie de nouveau, avec un veuve, Ginevra Brancacci; il enregistre sa dot et commence dans son livre de famille une page pour l'enregistrement des enfants qu'il aura de Ginevra: rien moins que onze (quatre garçons et sept filles), de 1404 à 1419, quand Ginevra meurt, elle aussi en accouchant, Goro refait les comptes de la dot reçue (pas moins de mille florins), et après il enregistre:

Et après cela il a été la volonté de Dieu de vouloir près de lui l'âme bénie de Ginevra, après le martyre d'une longue maladie par suite d'accouchement, qui a été supportée avec une merveilleuse force et patience (...). Que Dieu la bénisse, et qu'il nous donne beaucoup de patience, car son départ me fait un bien grand *dommage* ....[51]

En le 1421 Goro se remarie encore (il a alors soixante-et-un ans) pour la quatrième fois, avec Caterina Guicciardini; d'elle il aura en dix ans encore six enfants, sans compter un avortement.

Au total (mais c'est Goro lui-même qui fait ces comptes sur les pages de son livre de famille), l'infatigable marchand a provoqué rien moins que vingt-huit grossesses et causé la mort de trois femmes (même si indirectement). Il faut remarquer que de toute cette filiation, à cause de la mortalité enfantine et des fréquentes épidémies, pas plus de deux ou trois enfants, ne survécurent à Goro: dans le seul mois de juin 1420, six de ses enfants meurent chez lui.

8. De ces femmes vraies, qui se marient, transmettent d'un homme (le père) à un autre homme (le mari) leur dot, accouchent et meurent, de ces femmes

---

[50] Nos traductions de: "Da poi se n'andò a paradiso la mia donna Isabetta (...) sicchè di lei non posso avere a scrivere più figliuoli. Sia benedetto Idio. Son nati della Betta e di me otto, cioè 5 maschi e 3 femine." (G. Dati, *op. cit.*, p. 40)

[51] "Da poi è stato piacere di Dio volere apresso di sè l'anima benedetta della Ginevra, con martirio di lunga infirmità di parto, la quale à comportata con meravigliosa fortezza e paciencia (...). Dio la benedica, e a noi dia buona paciencia, chè grandissimo danno recevo de sua partita..." (*ibidem*, p. 93).

tragiquement réduites à des *épouses*, les pages des livres de famille sont remplies, mais la littérature établie et qui est à part ne nous parle pas d'elles, et l'on pourrait chercher en vain une trace de leur existence (c'est à dire de l'existence d'au moins la moitié de l'humanité) dans les siècles de notre littérature.

Le couple idéal de la littérature amoureuse coexiste côte à côte avec le couple réel des livres de familles (qui pourtant l'a engendré!), sans jamais le rencontrer, comme la réalité à côté d'un rêve, parce que ces deux couples s'inspirent de deux statuts différents et s'expriment à travers des codes tout à fait indépendants.

Le cas de Bonaccorso Pitti (1354-1430), marchand (mais aussi vaillant aventurier) auteur d'un livre de *Ricordi*[52] qui est en même temp une autobiographie et un livre d'aventures est significatif: Pitti vit une histoire d'amour qui paraît prise telle quelle des pages d'un roman courtois, il offre ses hommages à une femme qu'il connaît à peine en se déclarant "tout à elle"; et elle, en plaisantant, lui dit: "puisque tu es à moi, m'obéirais-tu si je te commandais?" Bonaccorso lui répond: "Essayez, et commandez". La femme alors lui commande d'aller à Rome pour l'amour d'elle; il s'agit d'une requête pratiquement impossible parce que (on est en le 1377) Florence est en guerre contre le Pape. Bonaccorso obéit au commandement au risque de sa vie en mettant quelques semaines pour aller et revenir.[53]

Et pourtant, le même Bonaccorso décrit de cette manière son mariage:

> J'arrivai à Florence et je pris la décision de me marier. Et, comme Guido di messire Tomaso di Neri del Palagio était l'homme le plus important et le plus estimé de Florence, je décidai de recevoir ma femme de ses mains, celle qu'il aurait choisie, *pourvu qu'elle fût de sa famille*.[54]

Et ainsi, par la médiation d'un courtier de mariages, Bonaccorso Pitti épouse sans problèmes la femme que désigne Guido del Palagio, l'homme qu'il a choisi comme parent (la fille d'un de ses cousines). Et quelques pages après il note sur son livre les systèmes les plus efficaces pour que sa femme donne naissance à des enfants mâles.

---

[52] Bonaccorso Pitti, *Ricordi*, dans *Mercanti scrittori...*, *cit.*, pp. 341-503.

[53] *Ibidem*, pp. 368-9.

[54] Notre traduction de: "Giunsi a Firenze e deliberai di torre moglie. E, sendo Guido di messer Tomaso di Neri del Palagio il maggiore e più creduto uomo di Firenze, diliberai di torla per le sue mani e qualunche a lui piacesse, *pure ch'ella fusse sua parente...*" *ibidem*, p. 392.

Pour confirmer *a contrario* la contradiction entre le code littéraire du couple et celui de la réalité matrimoniale, il est très intéressant de remarquer que le hiatus que nous avons vu dans la conduite du florentin cultivé Bonaccorso Pitti, est beaucoup moins grand, (et même peut être n'existe-il pas du tout), chez les écrivains qui ne possèdent pas par leur ignorance même, le code littéraire de l'amour courtois; pour ces cas (aussi rares que significatifs) on peut lire sur les pages mêmes des livres de famille, des phrases d'amour passionné pour la femme *réelle*.

Ainsi le maçon de Bologna Gaspare Nadi (1418-1500 environ) presque analphabète, qui a appris à lire et à écrire pendant son service chez un gentilhomme (et qui est un exemple des écrivains les moins cultivés, et dont nous conservons, par hasard, les traces dans un livre), s'abandonne, sans gêne, sur les pages de son livre de famille[55] à une déchirante lamentation pour la mort de son épouse adorée Cathalina (morte en 1461 d'un avortement après sa onzième grossesse, et six avortements, en seize ans de mariage):

... j'ai fait tout mon impossible (sic) pour la sauver parce que je l'amais autant qu'il était possible d'aimer parce que je ne crois pas qu'existe ou qu'ait jamais existé une femme meilleure qu'elle que dieu sauve son âme; elle fut ensevelie (...) avec tout l'honneur que j'ai pu lui donner et je prie dieu pour sa miséricorde et vous qui lisez pour que vous disiez un je vous salue marie pour son âme je vous salue marie...[56]

Cette lamentation funèbre (sans aucune majuscule et ponctuation comme tout le livre de Nadi) nous renvoie à un élément d'une importance extraordinaire; il existe aussi dans les livres de famille quelque trouée d'intériorité et d'affectivité, c'est à dire des passages où même les marchands occupent *l'espace d'écriture*, ouvert par l'exigence d'"écrire toujours tout", avec une écriture personnelle, psychologique, souvent bouleversante et émouvante. Ces trouées sont d'un grand intérêt littéraire, parce que elles marquent l'origine du journal intime, et de l'autobiographie, quelques siècles avant Jean-Jacques Rousseau.

Ces trouées coïncident souvent avec l'enregistrement sur le livre de famille

[55] G. Nadi, *Diario bolognese*, par C. Ricci et A. Bacchi Della Lega, Bologna, Romagnoli, 1886.

[56] Notre traduction de: "... yo li fie' quelo che meffò imposibole per champarla perchè yo l'amava quanto fose imposibole perchè non credo che nè sia nè fose mae una migiore de lie dio li faza passe a l'anema fo sepelida (...) chon quelo onore che me fo imposibole priego dio li dia paradisso per la soa piatà e missrechuodia e chosì el faza anchora ve priego voi che legiti le desside una avemaria per l'anema soa avemaria cracia plena" (*ibidem*, p. 52).

de la mort des personnes les plus chères; par exemple Giovanni di Paolo Morelli ouvre son coeur, après la mort de son fils aîné et chéri Alberto (1406),
avec une douleur tellement aiguë qu'elle le surprend avant tout lui même:

> Je n'aurais jamais imaginé que pour avoir séparé Dieu de moi, mon garçon
> ci-nommé, passant de cette vie à une autre, m'aurait fait éprouver et me
> ferait éprouver encore un si cruel couteau (…) ni moi, ni sa mère ne pou-
> vons l'oublier: nous avons toujours son image devant les yeux, et nous nous
> rappelons toutes ses manières, ses façons, et ses mots et ses gestes, le jour,
> la nuit, au déjeuner, au dîner, chez nous, dans la rue, en dormant, en veil-
> lant, à la campagne, à Florence; et à chaque moment un couteau nous perce
> le coeur….[57]

Il est très significatif qu'au moment même d'une douleur si cruelle, Giovanni Morelli s'abandonne à une véritable autoanalyse psychologique, pleine de remords
et d'auto-conscience, véritable crise de conscience, qui ne se résoud que par le
récit d'un rêve, riche de significations, autant religieuses que psychologiques.

9. En conclusion: on peut dire que le *duo* idéal des amoureux dont nous parle
la littérature se construit d'une manière tout à fait autonome, et même *en
opposition* par rapport au couple réel du mari et de la femme (de là, peut-être
la difficulté et le retard avec lesquels s'affirme le même terme synthétique et
dense de "couple").
   Mais plus encore: (comme on l'a vu) l'extrême difficulté/impossibilité de
parler directement de/à une femme réelle, sur laquelle repose, avec la poésie
d'amour, toute la littérature italienne, nous pousse à supposer que la littérature se
constitue en tant que telle (c'est à dire comme discours non-référentiel, autonome, comme fin en lui-même et source de plaisir en lui-même) justement *pour
ne pas* parler de la femme réelle, mais pour permettre à l'homme de parler de
lui-même, et mieux encore de s'imaginer, en se reflétant dans l'image créée par
lui, de la femme déformée et même renversée comme dans un miroir.

---

[57] "Non arei mai potuto istimare che l'avere Idio doviso da me il mio sopra iscritto figliuolo,
passando di questa vita ad altra, mi fusse suto e mi sia sì gravoso coltello (…) non si può
per me, nè eziandio pella madre dimenticare: ma di continuo abbiamo la sua immagine
innanzi, di tutti i modi, le condizioni, le parole e' suoi fatti ricordandoci, il dì, la notte, a
disinare, a cena, in casa, fuori, dormendo, vegghiando, in villa, in Firenze; e in ogni forma
che noi istiamo e' ci tiene un coltello che ci passa il cuore…" (G. Morelli, *op. cit.*, p. 295;
notre traduction).

The Making of the Couple
in Old and Middle English Literature

By JAN W. DIETRICHSON, *University of Oslo.*

The topic of my paper is wide and somewhat problematic in the sense that of all the many literary texts that are left us from medieval England, we find a broad and coherent discussion of marital relationships only in Chaucer's *Canterbury Tales*, which Professor Brewer is to deal with. There exist, however, a number of treatises containing af fairly extensive discussion of such relationships. I have included a few examples of such semi-literary material in my paper.

Since Anglo-Saxon writers paid hardly any attention to such themes as love and marriage, I have had to focus my attention on the period from 1100 to 1500, the main emphasis falling on thirteenth- and fourteenth-century texts. I have had to consult many texts and have found a little here, and a little there. Therefore my paper has become a kind of mosaic, out of which, hopefully, certain patterns may emerge. The question I put to my material was whether and how the outlook on marital relationships changed, but I have had trouble finding an answer. The uncertainty of dating makes it difficult to order these mostly anonymous texts within a line of development. There is an almost complete absence of short form prose narratives within the two periods I intend to cover; this has necessitated a selection of texts from a fairly broad range of other genres. I have tried to make this selection as representative as possible, but have obviously found it impossible to cover *all* the relevant material.

My intention is to focus on the marital norms and values that are reflected in my texts. What motives led men and women to marry, and how do husband and wife relate to each other within the marriage? Is the husband always assumed to be the dominant partner? Is marriage possible across social boundaries, and how does an inequality of social background affect matrimonial relations? To what extent does a monastic ideal of asceticism and chastity make itself felt in these texts? Do they present marriage as a necessary, but second-rate way of life? How important are good sexual relations for the success of the marriage? These are some of the questions that I hope my texts will help me answer.

In the preface to his book on *The Medieval Idea of Marriage* Christopher N.L. Brooke says that since he first had the notion of writing a history of medieval marriage in 1962, "the history of marriage has been a major growth area in historical studies, and medieval marriage has had its share."[1] A little further on he is certain that the novels of Jane Austin tell us nothing of the social or economic pressures on factory girls, but much about motives – including the motive to marry – that affected choice and opportunity in her day.[2] His argument is relevant for my material as well: literary texts can hardly be considered reliable as direct sources of political, economic, or social history. But they take us into human minds, acquainting us with feelings and motives – why, for instance, medieval men and women married and what marriage meant to them. This is an area which documentary or archeological sources will not tell us much about. In this sense an exploration of literary evidence may be a contribution to social history as well.

The Anglo-Saxon Period

In *A Study of Old English Literature* C.L. Wrenn places Anglo-Saxon literature in a wider Germanic context:

> Old English poetry has only the slightest treatment of love, and that almost impersonal.... As a poetic theme love is practically alien to the Germanic, and therefore to the Anglo-Saxon genius. For, as we learn very early from Tacitus's *Germania*, marriage is a practical, not an emotionally egocentric affair with the ancient Germanic peoples from whose stock the Anglo-Saxons had sprung, and among whom, he tells us, *Sera iuvenum venus* – young men's falling in love comes late.[3]

The truth of Professor Wrenn's statement is amply confirmed by the poverty of my material from the period 700-1100. Marriage was simply too trivial a topic in the heroic age for the scops to consider it a theme suitable for song. It was taken for granted as a practical, every-day arrangement. We do have, however, two short poems telling us about the love of spouses for each other.

The title of "The Wife's Lament" was given to the poem by later scribes, who assumed that it is a lament of a woman separated from her husband and surrounded by enemies. It is remarkable that she is allowed to express herself with a touching emotion in a dramatic monologue, and equally remarkable that we are

---

1   Christopher N.L. Brooke, *The Medieval Idea of Marriage* (Oxford Press, 1989), p. vii.

2   Brooke, p. 4.

3   C.L. Wrenn, *A Study of Old English Literature* (London, 1967), p. 21.

able to follow the ebb and flow of her feelings. The words she is using for her husband tell us quite a bit about her relationship to him: "hlaford", "leod-fruma" (lord, prince). She harbours antagonistic feelings against the false kinsmen who keep her apart from the man she loves, and feels miserable remembering how her beloved lord put her away in a cavern in the earth. She is angry with him as well for having left her behind. Finally she expresses great sorrow for him having to endure hardship in a country far away. One is impressed by the love and loyalty of the woman, who has let herself be guided by the man she accepts without question as her lord and master.

"The Husband's Message" (or "The Lover's Message") probably expresses a husband's warm feelings for his absent wife. This poem exists in the form of a speech made by a piece of wood on which apparently is carved a message from a husband (or lover) to his lady. He has been separated from her by a feud, but has overcome his difficulties in a land across the sea and is eager to assure her of his faithfulness and to welcome her in his new home.

It is a significant fact that women play a completely secondary role in the greatest Anglo-Saxon heroic poem, *Beowulf*, as they do in the *Chanson de Roland*. Most notable is the Danish queen Wealtheow, wife of King Hrothgar. The poem underlines her nobility and importance: in the hall she is seated beside the king adorned with gold, and she is allowed to welcome Beowulf, to reward him after the fight with Grendel, and to speak freely to her lord, reminding him of what is expected of whoever wants to be remembered as a good and worthy ruler. The text says nothing directly about her marriage, but we can infer from it both her loyalty to Hrothgar and her lofty social position almost equal to his. She is also mentioned as a guarantee that peace will exist between the Danes and her own tribe, the Hemings.

Not every woman in *Beowulf* is loyal and generous. We hear of the terrible queen Thryth, who had those who dared look her directly in the face killed. When she marries, her husband Offa puts a stop to this. In her case marriage has a salutary effect, for on Offa's throne she becomes celebrated for her goodness. She marries on the advice of her father, while Hrothgar arranges the marriage of his daughter Freawaru to the good-looking Prince Ingeld of the Heathobards to end the bitter strife between the Danes and the Heathobards. Arranged marriages for political purposes are not unknown to the *Beowulf* poet. The poem tells us something about how marriages might be established and about the strong position of the wife in aristocratic marriage – almost on a par with her husband – but little else.

The Middle English Period

The themes of love and marriage gained new prominence in the Middle English period partly due to French influence taking root after the Norman Conquest. The Continental concept of courtly love created by the troubadours from the eleventh century onwards was brought to England by Frenchmen, but modified here in the sense that the aspiring lover no longer found his reward in devoted service to his lady, but sought fulfilment in marriage. The English metrical romances also tell us that women now seemed much more prominent in the minds of the poets: devotion and fidelity to the lady now became a major obligation for the knight. When W.F. Bolton argues that much medieval love poetry is ideal and theoretical, he certainly has a good point.[4]

French courtly romances were translated or imitated by Englishmen from the thirteenth century. This new type of text in English reflects an important social fact of Post-Norman-Conquest England: landless Frenchmen married well-born Englishwomen. Marriage was both a means of satisfying sexual appetites and of acquiring wealth, status, and honour as well.[5] These ideals are reflected in the English courtly romances.

A third tendency may be seen in religious texts of a moralistic nature: marriage is presented as a way of life that comes out second best when compared to virginal chastity. This fact is easy to understand when we remind ourselves that the art of writing was mainly restricted to clerics or monks living under an obligation of celibacy. In the Middle Ages marriage became a part of the religious life of Christendom – visible, for instance, in the fact that it was taken out of secular courts and brought into the courts of the Church – but it had always a secular, earthly, and physical element as well, which was in apparent conflict with the celibate ideal. To Brooke, this is a central fact about the legal history of marriage in our period.[6] However, in its late years sexual union became more accepted as of the essence of marriage even to the theologians.[7] According to Christian doctrine marriage had for a long time been a sacrament between the partners, monogamous and consecrated.[8] John Wycliffe (1328-84), for instance, adapted a tolerant attitude to matrimony in a short treatise called *Of Wedded Men and Wives and Of Their Children.*[9]

---

4   *The Middle Ages*, ed. W.F. Bolton; vol. I of *History of Literature in the English Language* (London, 1970), p. 245.

5   Bolton, p. 71.

6   Brooke, pp. 21-22.

7   Brooke, p. 132.

8   Brooke, p. 201.

An excellent example of the stern clerical view of marriage is an anonymous prose exhortation to virginity called *Holy Maidenhood*.[10] The writer warns believers against marriage and fleshly lust. The sins of the body sully a woman, and therefore the virgin will always be morally superior to the married woman. We get a graphic account of the disadvantages of matrimony including the physical suffering that pregnancy entails: the head aches, the breasts are burdened with milk, and her pain deprives the woman of a sound night's sleep. That husband and wife are bound to quarrel, the text takes for granted.

The Ancrene Riwle is an anonymous treatise written in the early decades of the thirteenth century for the guidance of young women who wanted to live as anchoresses.[11] Like *Holy Maidenhood* it upholds the ideal of virginity, explaining at length how anchoresses may protect themselves from falling victim to fleshly sin. The text is not much concerned with marriage, but it contains a suggestive analogy, indicating that the husband has the right to govern his wife. It instructs him, also, how he may break in a newly-wedded wife by pretending to be stern so as to correct the faults he finds in her. When her love has been tested in this manner and she is well disciplined, everything will turn to joy! What to us sounds like pure male chauvinism was perhaps more acceptable in the thirteenth century.[12]

Relevant in the present context are the many parental instructions to children written in the Middle Ages. A good example is *The Good Wife Taught Her Daughter* (earliest text ca. 1350), a poem characterized by its editor T.F. Mustanoja as "one of the first works extant in European literature that are addressed especially to middle class women."[13] It shows that finding a suitable husband for her daughter was a constant concern for the medieval mother. Since there were more women than men, not every woman was able to marry. Characteristically, in one version of the poem the mother concludes that daughters should be given to men as soon as they are of age.[14]

Here the mother is indebted to the teachings of the Church and to popular no-

---

9   John Wycliffe, *Of Weddid Men and Wifes and Of Here Children*, abstract in J.E. Wells, *A Manual of the Writings in Middle English. 1050-1400* (New Haven, Conn., 1926), p. 472. See also, *A Literary History of England*, ed. Albert C. Baugh (New York, 1948), p. 271.

10 *Hali Meiðhad*. ed. A.F. Colborn (Copenhagen, 1940).

11 I have used *The Ancrene Riwle*, trans. M.B. Salu (London, 1955).

12 Salu, p. 97.

13 *The Good Wife Taught Her Daughter*, ed. Tauno F. Mustanoja, Annales Academiæ Scientiarum Fennicæ, B LXI. 2 (Helsinki, 1948).

14 Mustanoja, p. 171, l. 183.

tions of a woman's position in society for what she can teach her daughter. The young woman is encouraged to be submissive to her husband, to answer him meekly, and to love him above all things. She should work hard, look after her servants, be thrifty, and chastise her children when they need it. *The Good Wife Taught Her Daughter* presents, then, a moderate and reasonable set of bourgeois norms, well adapted to her future station in life. The mother assumes that her daughter will marry a person of means, and that her future husband will be good to her if she is prudent in her daily life and meets her obligations to him. Marriage seems to be a practical arrangement of great value to both spouses, not least the wife. The mother, however, is not much concerned with its emotional aspect.

The Good Wife Taught Her Daughter has a companion text, *How the Wise Man Taught His Son*, surviving in four manuscripts from the fifteenth century.[15] The father warns his son against marrying for money and advises him to chastise his wife with love – i.e. the tongue – and not the rod. He takes it for granted that a wife should be subordinate to her husband, but emphasizes that she must be respected and treated well. His moderate and reasonable attitude is similar to that of the mother in *The Good Wife Taught Her Daughter*.

The delightful thirteenth century debate poem *The Owl and the Nightingale* contains a fairly broad discussion of problems relating to love and matrimony. In the course of the dispute between the two birds the owl accuses the nightingale of having tempted a lady to sin through her song. The nightingale answers back that she will only incite women to virtuous love:

> Indeed, you evil thing, you lie
> Through me no marriage vows could die,
> But true it is I sing and stray
> Where ladies and fair maidens play;
> And true it is of love I sing,
> For woman wedded with a ring
> May better love a husband dear
> Than other lover anywhere.[16]

The bird knows that her song is good, but that it may be made to serve deeds that do not conform to the regulations of the Church. She is tolerant of romantic love, even out of wedlock; such illicit love may, after all, be regularized by marriage and the spouses be happy ever after. Through his song, the nightingale avers, women are made to see that "foolish love can ne'er last long"(p. 51). She

---

15 Cf. Mustanoja, pp. 63-65.

16 *The Owl and the Nightingale*, trans. Graydon Eggers (Durham, N.C., 1955), p. 50.

cannot understand how any man can wrong a worthy man in his bed, seducing his wedded wife.

The owl is sympathetic to ill-treated wives who avenge themselves on their husbands. Men who fornicate with other women, leaving their wives threadbare at home, only get what they deserve when their wives cuckold them. But when husbands love and keep their wives aright, their good wives will return their love in kind. Both birds, then, assume as a matter of course that a normal, happy marriage is the best type of enduring relationship that adult men and women can enter into. The subordinate position of the female is made explicit: wives are expected to serve their husbands in bed and at board, "With gracious deed and gentle word..." (p. 55), but husbands have their obligations, too, which they have to meet if they want their spouses to remain faithful. The poem realistically stresses the importance of the sexual side of marriage. Both birds disapprove of fornication and adultery as a menace to the stability of marriage. The owl, in particular, makes husbands responsible if their wives go astray, but does not recognize that sometimes the weaker sex is to blame.

I shall next discuss three well-known courtly poems that were written by anonymous poets from the thirteenth century onwards. Most prominently these romances describe the process whereby mere acquaintance develops into love and love into marriage, which comes as a happy ending. What comes after marriage is often less interesting: it is assumed to be a happy and stable relationship that the poet needs not say much about. This fact does not make these poems uninteresting from our viewpoint.

King Horn (ca. 1250) is usually considered to be the earliest English verse romance.[17] Horn is of royal birth; having been driven away by Saracens from his own kingdom of Suddene, he is adopted by the royal court of Westernesse and instructed in courtly duties. Here the king's daughter Rimenhild falls desperately in love with him. It is remarkable that the text does not censure her for her aggressiveness in love: she actively woos the young hero, not caring what people might think of her. Her initiative is usually considered to indicate a pre-courtly ethic.[18] Horn courteously puts her off, telling her that he is born a thrall. Implied is of course that a union with him would dishonour her. Now he wants to advance his honour in war before he takes a wife. He persuades her to make her father dub him a knight, enabling him to win in battle in Ireland the honour he needs to be worthy of her. As we can tell, the love theme illustrates well the demands of the courtly marriage code: for the hero, in particular, high

---

[17] In Walter H. French, *Essays on King Horn* (Ithaca, New York, 1940), pp. 153-204.

[18] Bolton, p. 75.

rank is not sufficient; he must also prove through deeds of prowess that he is worthy of his high-born bride.

The late thirteenth century romance *Havelok* does not conform entirely to the conventional pattern: hero and heroine fall in love at the beginning, and after many trials and much suffering they marry in the end.[19] In this instance, the hero is heir to the throne of Denmark. Dispossessed of his heritage by an unfaithful guardian, young Havelok is brought to Grimsby by a fisherman. He becomes the kitchen-boy in the household of Godrich, the treacherous guardian of Goldeborough, who is heiress to the English throne. Assuming that the kitchen-boy is a serf, Godrich will force Havelok and Goldeborough to marry. By feudal law, when a woman marries a serf, she forfeits her claim to land. Arranging a marriage of this kind, Godrich will therefore be able to cheat the princess of her heritage. Lacking the means to support a wife, Havelok refuses to marry, but yields finally to Godrich's threats. In Goldeborough's case we see what a terrible social stigma it is for her to marry a thrall. She is mournful because of the dishonour done to her, but is consoled when Havelok's royal origins are revealed to her by magical means. Both his lineage and his prowess make him a worthy mate for his high-born spouse. The poem shows that even in a marriage arranged by force against the will of the two involved, love may grow and finally turn the relationship into an ideal union. We find here the same idealization of marriage that we have seen before, as well as a realistic appraisal of a good sexual relationship as being essential for marital success.

In the late fifteenth century romance *The Squire of Low Degree* a young squire loves the daughter of the king of Hungary.[20] She loves him in return, but there is an obstacle to matrimony: though a gentleman, he is not rich. For the sake of their mutual honour she asks him to prove his manhood in battle. When informed by a false steward that the princess is willing to marry the squire, the king does not punish her wooer:

> For I have seen that many a page
> Have become men by marriage;
> Then it is seemly that [the] squire
> To have my daughter in this manner (p. 733).

Only if he tries to seduce her will he be put to death. Assailed by the steward

---

19 *Havelok*, ed. G.V. Smithers (Oxford, 1987).

20 *In Middle English Metrical Romances*, I-II, eds. Walter Hoyt French and Charles Brockway Hale (New York, 1964), vol. II, pp. 721-55.

with thirty-three armed men during a tryst, the squire slays the steward plus seven other enemies. He is then arrested and put in prison. Convinced that her lover is dead, the princess is faithful to the extent of keeping what she believes to be his dead body in her room for seven years! In the meantime the king releases the young man, having promised him his daughter and land after his knightly journey abroad. He sets out on his quest, proves his courage and returns to Hungary and his beloved as a hero. The story ends, of course, with their wedding festivities. It affirms the validity of the aristocratic ideals of honour, valour, and faithful love, and it indicates, also, that a moral superiority makes it possible for a person of low rank to aspire even to a royal marriage. It is inherent worth that really counts. As in Chaucer's *Knight's Tale*, marriage becomes a reward for those who stand the test of adversity.

The three romances that I have discussed throw light on the emotional and social background of medieval aristocratic marriage from several important angles. Behind much of what is being said we sense a courtly marriage code. To marry right is a matter of honour: the spouses should preferably be of equal rank. But *The Squire of Low Degree* indicates that low rank and lack of means might be compensated for by high moral qualities. In the texts I have chosen, the heroes and heroines all possess such qualities, for which reason their marriages are successful. Their moral stature has to be tested, for instance in battle. A young man who passes the test may marry so that he rises in society. Marriage as a cause of social mobility only reflects a fact of medieval English society, as we have seen. Those who climb in this manner become the legal masters of their high-born mates. But the subjection of wives to the will of their husbands is not made much of by these texts; they imply rather that man and wife exist as equal partners with the husband as the *primus inter pares*. This was how the poets thought it had to be in aristocratic or royal families. The picture of marriage that the three romances convey is an idyllic one, the mutual love and loyalty of the spouses being taken for granted. But what leads up to marriage is not always so idyllic. In *Havelok* the evil Godrich uses matrimony for the wrong purposes, furthering his own political ends by forcing two young people who do not know or love each other, to marry, The poem tells us, however, that even an arranged union of this kind may succeed if the spouses are of the right sort.

John Gower's unobtrusive manner of writing in his major poem on the nature of love, *Confessio Amantis* (ca. 1390), should not obscure the fact that he has wise things to say about marriage. Its framework is a confession of a penitent lover, Amans, to his confessor Genius, who stands for such key virtues as

Measure and Reason.[21] In the course of their exchanges the Confessor uses a large number of stories – most of them drawn from Ovid – as exempla to support the sound moral advice he wants to give his listener. In one of them shrewish Xantippe scolds Socrates for not doing his share of the housework. Her anger stirred, she pours a pot of water over his head. The poor man just sits there by the fire till his clothes are dry, saying nothing: "In which he acted for the best,/ And earned himself a little rest."[22] The story recommends harassed husbands to be patient with their wives, but does not consider the possibility that the matter might be seen from Xantippe's viewpoint too! The tale of Pygmalion illustrates the value of sexual activity in marriage. Thanks to the goddess Venus, the sculptor wins himself "a lusty wife/ Able and ready to his will. ... All he desired, he found abed..." (pp. 152-53). Marriage is presented as a natural way of life: men and maidens should all make haste to love and wed. But the poem also contains a long passage in praise of virginity, which the Confessor finds lovely in itself. He warns against jealousy in marriage: men who become jealous are insufficiently virile. They spend their lives spying on their ladies, so that both spouses have to exist in loveless misery. Finally Venus herself warns Amans against love in old age. Compared to the romances, *Confessio Amantis* deals with problems of love and marriage on a more everyday and practical level. We are no longer in the rarefied atmosphere of courtly love.

William Langland's long allegorical poem *The Vision of Piers Plowman* exists in three versions written between the 1360s and the second half of the 1380s.[23] This great work is both a biting socio-political satire and a comprehensive presentation of the variety of human experience, including, inevitably, a commentary on the function of marriage. The latter is mainly to be found in the second part of the poem, the *Vita*.

Here the dreamer asks what it means to do well, to do better, and to do best, eliciting from his informants, Thought, Wit, Study et cetera the moral elucidation of the whole allegory. Wit is the one concerned with marriage: "Those who live truly wedded in this world are Do Well;/ For they must work and win and be the world's sustenance" (p. 108). Wit's words show us what a high value Langland attaches to matrimony: it has been established by the will of God and is therefore a sacred institution. It is a natural state of existence for most men and women and the basis of human material life. For it is wedded people who have to toil so that all may eat every day. However, all those who lead a life of

---

21   Cf. J.A.W. Bennett, *Middle English Literature* (Oxford, 1986), p. 420.

22   John Gower, *Confessio Amantis*, trans. Terence Tiller (Harmondsworth, 1963), p. 135.

23   I have used William Langland, *The Vision of Piers Plowman*, trans. Henry H. Wells (London, 1959).

continence and contemplation are more beloved by the Lord than those "who follow as the flesh leads" (p. 218). The poet, then, upholds the monastic ideal of chastity and abstinence, but is realistic enough to understand that it is only for the chosen few.

He is extremely intolerant of all those who are born out of wedlock, and particularly of the sinful offspring of incestuous unions. Honest people are legitimately conceived, while "false and faithless folk, thieves and liars,/ Wasters and wretchers, are not from wedlock, I assure you..." (p. 109). In a moralistic tone Langland argues that guilt and grief come of unnatural marriages entered into for materialistic reasons. Only those should wed who are suited for each other; love, not land, is the proper inducement to marriage. This is completely in line with his general tendency to inveigh against the greed of his times.

Matrimony is not always idyllic: we learn, for instance, that a husband may be forced to flee from his own house to escape the revilings of a wicked wife. One senses a strong feeling of compassion in the poem for "poor folk in hovels,/ Charged with children and overcharged by landlords" (p. 92). The hard lives of the indigent are described in moving terms, expressive of the personal experience lying behind Langland's words here.

The lives of the poor we see at close range in *The Second Shepherds' Play* (ca. 1385) as well.[24] In this fine mystery play most of the text is given to a comic subplot of the couple Mak and Gill. At the outset a shepherd, Coll, complains of the peasant's hard lot, exploited as he is by wealthy landlords, while his colleague Gib feels that wedded men have not their own will; they lead hard lives, but say nothing against it. His wife is sharp as a thistle, has eyebrows like pig's bristles, and a sour-looking face! Marriage will bring you to grief, he warns young men, so you better stay away from it. His misogynic complaint is clearly humorous and not to be taken too seriously. The same is true of Mak's description to Coll of his better half: she lies lounging by the fire, drinks well and eats as fast as she can, and every year she produces a baby and some years two. When Mak later comes home to his wife, we are allowed to see her side of the picture and recognize then that his description of her is too subjective to be true. Behind his plaintive words looms a social reality, that is, the hardship of toiling husbands, trying to feed and clothe their ever-growing families. For the play reflects, also, the traditional division of labour within the family with the husband working for wages outside the house and the wife at home with the children.

---

[24] In *The Norton Anthology of English Literature*, I-II, ed. M.H. Abrams, 3rd ed. (New York, 1974), I, pp. 375-95.

Conclusion

As a result of the teachings of the English Church in the late Anglo-Saxon period, fornication and adultery had by the tenth century become crimes against God,
and therefore offences to both Church and state.[25] Henceforth matrimony was a
sacred institution, established by the will of God. This basic Church doctrine is
taken for granted in all the texts I have dealt with. In almost all of them marriage is
seen as the normal and natural way of life for most men and women. Monastic
asceticism, chastity, and contemplation may be an ideal state of existence, but is
clearly only for God's few elect. Some of the texts recognize that fornication
and adultery do occur, but see these phenomena as regrettable deviations from
the norm of the Church. A regular marital relationship is always preferable.
Though tolerant of illicit love, even the nightingale must admit that "foolish love
can ne'er last long."[26] Her attitude is not very different from that of the Church,
which recognized betrothal followed by intercourse as a valid marriage con-
tract.[27] The fact that we have only one true fabliau before Chaucer, a humorous
narrative poem titled *Dame Sirith* (ca. 1250),[28] may also indicate that medieval
English writers found marriage too serious a matter to trifle with.

In my texts, matrimony is presented as a necessary social institution, that may
offer the individual much satisfaction, but also be a source of sorrow and toil.
One of them, *The Good Wife Taught Her Daughter*, especially points to the strong
need for a young woman to marry, simply, we must take it, for the maintenance
that a husband was able to give her. A nunnery might be her only alternative
means of subsistence.

It would give a false impression to suggest that marriage is depicted as a
purely practical arrangement in my material. There are, on the contrary, several
texts that emphasize mutual respect and love as its only true basis. The courtly
romances in particular make much of the *emotional* bonds between a man and a
woman before and in marriage. It is a striking fact, nontheless, that so much of
my material is concerned with the qualities needed to make marriage a success in
terms of practical everyday living. Its element of moral reasoning and sound
advice is notable. The same can be said for its realistic appraisal of human

---

[25] Cf. Lawrence Stone, *The Family, Sex and Marriage in England 1500-1800* (London,
1977), p. 498.

[26] *The Owl and the Nightingale*, p. 51.

[27] Cf. Stone, p. 628.

[28] In *Middle English Humorous Tales in Verse*, ed. George H. McKnight (New York,
1972).

nature, visible, for instance, in the frank avowal of erotic longing that members of both sexes are allowed to express. The fact that several of my texts appreciate how important a harmonious sexual life really is in marriage, points in the same direction. Victorian prudishness is an unknown matter in medieval literature!

A logical consequence of this appreciation is the warning against "unnatural marriages" – i.e. marriage for money or land or where the difference in age is great – that we find in Gower and Langland. That the impotence of an aging husband may alienate him from his wife and turn him into a cuckold, both Chaucer (*The Merchant's Tale*) and Boccaccio (*Decameron*, ii, 10) are aware of.

My texts vary considerably in their presentation of the relationship of the spouses within the marriage, from the subjection of the wife to the will of the husband that we find in *The Ancren Riwle* to a situation closer to equality in the courtly romances. The general assumption is, however, that the husband is the head of the household and thus the leading party in marriage, to whom the wife owes loyalty, respect, and – in the last instance – obedience. Even the stubborn and irritable wife in a miracle play I have not discussed, *The Towneley Play of Noah* (ca. 1475),[29] enters the Ark and thus submits herself to the will of Noah in the end, just in time to avoid death by drowning. There are no strongwilled and vindictive wives, like Hallgerd in the *Njal's Saga*, actively working against the interests of their husbands, in the texts I have consulted.

If wives have obligations to their husbands, so do husbands to their wives. This view is expressed most clearly, perhaps, in *The Owl and the Nightingale*, where the owl explains how dire the consequences may be for husbands who do not treat their wives as they should. The wise man's advice to his son to chastise his wife with love and not the rod equally testifies to the respect for the married woman and understanding of her feelings that characterize some of my texts. It may surprise us today, however, that they hardly mention the fruit of marriage, children, and how they may contribute to the happiness and mutual love of the spouses. In *Havelok* the title hero and his queen can glory in fifteen children, the sons all kings and the daughters all queens, while poor Mak in *The Second Shepherds' Play* is complaining of his burden, having to feed his ever-increasing brood of children. A person's place in the social hierarchy and financial strength seem to decide, then, his feelings about his offspring. There is a world of difference, obviously, between the courtly romances, where material well-being is mostly taken for granted, and texts like *Piers Plowman* or the play just mentioned, where the struggle of the poor to feed and clothe themselves is described in sympathetic and even pathetic terms. But nowhere do we find any suggestion that poverty in itself may be the cause of dissension in marriage.

---

[29]   In *Fourteenth Century Verse & Prose*, ed. Kenneth Sisam (Oxford, 1950), pp. 185-203.

Marriage may have its storm and stress. A temperamental and shrewish wife can, for instance, make life unpleasant for her husband. She is a standard figure in medieval literature, exemplified in my material by Mrs. Noah and Gower's Xantippe. Still its underlying assumption is that even quarrelling spouses feel a deep-seated loyalty to each other. The possibility of divorce is not even hinted at. That divorces did occur in real life, is another matter; most commonly one spouse left his or her mate, to take another in the nearest village.[30]

Being mainly concerned with the process of courtship leading up to marriage, the courtly romances I have studied do not tell us anything about the relations of the spouses after the wedding ceremony is over beyond the trite "And then they lived happily ever after." But they do inform us well about the norms governing the establishment of an aristocratic marriage. Honour is the key word in this context, that is, a marriage should contribute to the public recognition of the individual worth of both the young people involved. Ideally this means equality of lineage, social rank, and financial situation. *The Squire of Low Degree* suggests, however, that it is perfectly possible for a young wooer to overcome obstacles such as low rank and a lack of means through military glory and being faithful to his high-born lady. It reflects an historical fact of medieval England that it is always *men* who rise in society in this manner. In the romances honour's requirements do not seem to conflict with inclination; particularly the happiness of a wife in marriage depends on the husband's being of the right sort. It is logical, therefore, that the high-born lady will not consider marrying a suitor of low rank till he has proven his worth in the field. To do otherwise would involve a lifelong humiliation.

Finally a few words about the nature of the family unit that my texts lead me to infer. The concept that best describes what we find here is, I believe, the Open Lineage Family. The term has been coined by Lawrence Stone, who defines the most striking features of this family type as its permeability by outside influences and its subordination of the individual's freedom of choice to the interests of others: lineage, kin, parents, neighbours. Inside the home the nuclear family was subordinated to the will of its head, its total amount of affective feelings was limited, and it was short-lived, being frequently dissolved by the death of one or both parents or by the early departure from home of the children. This was the characteristic family type in the sixteenth century and almost certainly a millennium before it, Stone maintains.[31] His pattern is clearly too schematized

---

[30] Cf. Henry Ansgar Kelly, *Love and Marriage in the Age of Chaucer* (Ithaca, 1974), p. 241, and Stone, p. 37.

[31] Cf. Stone, pp. 4-5.

to fit my material in every respect, but it is surprising how many of its features do. I will, for instance, point to the insistence on honour and lineage in the metrical romances, on the authority of the husband, the concern with the necessities of everyday living, the absence of the nuclear family unit in most of these texts, or the close affective bonds between parents and children that to our minds seem characteristic of family life. A concept like Stone's does not explain everything, but may still be useful in holding the disparate elements of my large material together in a comprehensive picture.

The Couple in Chaucer's Fabliaux

By DEREK BREWER, *Emmanuel College, Cambridge*

The married couple is the subject of the oldest recorded comic tale in the European tradition, that of the seduction of the goddess of love, Aphrodite, by the god of war, Ares, as told by Homer (*Odyssey, 8.266-366*). Aphrodite's husband, Hephaistos, the lame smith-god, entraps them in an invisible metal net when making love and shows them to the other gods. They laugh at all three, and Hermes expresses envy of the situation of Ares.

This story goes echoing down the ages, retold with variations of approval, disapproval and interpretation It has the basic elements of many of the traditional international comic tales of Europe. There is a marriage bond, which is infringed, a desirable wife, an ugly husband, an attractive and lively man. A wrong is done, and in that consists the comedy, but the moral tone is neutral, indulgent, or favouring the seducer. The husband loses honour; so does, in a different way, the wife, for their honour is as inseparably linked as they are, but the seducer does not.

The reception of the story is characterised by a certain amused detachment. No sympathy is felt for the husband, and only sufficient sympathy to allow imaginative enjoyment is felt for the lovers. Their embarrassment is derided and there is satisfaction in seeing the biter bit. The comedy depends on (a) the concept of the couple, with marriage as an exclusive sexual bond (for if Hephaistos had no legitimate claim to Aphrodite there would be no significance in Ares making love to her); (b) inequality of age and attractiveness between the married pair, (though it is always the husband who is old and unattractive, and there seem to be no examples of comic tales about a young man married to an old woman and being seduced by a vigorous young woman: the comedy of a young man married to an old or shrewish wife is of a quite different order); (c) a successful seduction; (d) discovery, or recognition, or publication, if only the story itself.

The indissolubly bonded sexual couple, with inherent or adventitious inequalities between the partners, has for many many centuries provided the basis for comedy in literature. The sexual couple focuses personal concerns perhaps more sharply than any other human grouping. This was particularly so in the Middle Ages, when marriage, except for the very highest and richest, was indissoluble.

Marriage being concerned with the large themes of sexuality, procreation, education, personal responsibility, property, inheritance, was the subject of intense legal debate and much legislation.[1] Although so personal, marriage cannot be the private concern of two individuals only; it concerns social and public structures in various ways. For this reason it is inevitably a subject for legislation, even in modern times when the sacred aspect of marriage and its indissolubility have been largely abandoned in advanced industrial societies. But its indissolubility in medieval times is the crucial element. It seems unlikely that there will be so many jokes about the married couple in the future. There will be no need for them.

One of the functions of jokes is to express our resentment against the tyranny of regulation. Hence the widespread popularity of political jokes in Communist societies and their relative absence in democracies, where the political jokes in so far as they exist are of a different kind. But no jokes ever overthrew a dictatorship and the Romantic and Freudian view of the subversive nature of jokes, reiterated by a very distinguished social anthropologist[2] needs to be qualified. The subversiveness of jokes, or even of satire, allows the oppressed to let off steam rather than to throw off the yoke. Jokes are a substitute for action because they promote imaginative action, allow the contemplation of alternatives, and so relieve oppression of feeling, if not of fact. Hence the moral neutrality, or the contemplative quality of the stories we shall be considering. Paradoxically the apparent subversiveness of jokes, by affording a channel for resentment, may support, or at least consent to, the established order. More certainly, such jokes *need* the established order in a very obvious way. Jokes about marriage need the existence of a firm authoritative institution of marriage.

It may be that such an institution, even if not monogamous, is inherent in human social structures, but it is even more deeply based on the biological absolutes of sexual drive, possessiveness and rivalry, which allow us to respond to Chaucer's *fabliaux* even though marital mores and concepts have now so greatly changed. The poems themselves embody many of their own assumptions.

Those *fabliaux* of Chaucer's which depend on recognition of the couple are *The Miller's Tale, The Reeve's Tale, The Merchant's Tale* and *The Shipman's Tale.* Other tales, and other poems, offer important insights.[3] At this stage it

1   R.M. Helmholz, *Marriage Litigation in Medieval England* (Cambridge, 1974). C.N.L. Brooke, *The Medieval Idea of Marriage* (Cambridge, 1989). J.A. Brundage, *Law, Sex and Christian Society in Medieval Europe* (Chicago and London, 1987). H.A. Kelly, *Love and Marriage in the Age of Chaucer* (Ithaca and London, 1975).

2   Mary Douglas, 'Jokes', *Implicit Meanings* (London, 1975). For a more schematic approach see M. Olsen, *Les Transformations du Triangle Erotique* (Copenhagen, 1976).

would be pedantic to query or abandon the wellrecognised generic term *'fabliaux'* for certain of Chaucer's poems. The French *fabliaux* offer a convenient generic analogue, hallowed by use, but Chaucer's poems have many differences from them.

In *The Miller's Tale* a student, Nicholas, lodging with an elderly jealous carpenter seduces his landlord's recently-married eighteen-year-old pretty wife, Alison. The student dupes the ignorant and simple-minded carpenter by a most improbable tale of the coming of a second Flood. To survive it, all three settle in tubs slung in the roof; the carpenter falls asleep, and Nicholas and Alison go to bed together. Eventually the carpenter is suddenly awakened by the effects of a subplot, comic in itself, cuts the rope that holds his tub, crashes to the ground, breaks his arm, and is mocked as a madman by Nicholas, Alison and his neighbours. A good deal of the humour lies in the absurd trick about the Flood, but the pleasure lies in the sympathetic enjoyment of Nicholas's sexual adventure and the holiday for the everyday conscience. The jealous old husband attracts no sympathy. We are all on the side of life. Nevertheless we also relish the nature of the discovery and the spectacle of the bitter bit which is presented both by the main plot and the sub-plot.

The sub-plot is another comic tale, whose nature is of some importance. Alison, a very pretty girl, is also wooed by the village dandy, called Absalon. When she and Nicholas are in bed together, Absalon comes to serenade her from outside her window. She tells him to go away. He asks for a kiss. She puts out of the window not her face but another portion of her anatomy, which he kisses with an enthusiasm which rapidly turns to fury. (This incidentally plays upon an ancient gross European insult.) He goes away to a friend of his, a smith, gets a red hot iron, then returns and asks for another kiss. This time Nicholas thinks the joke so exquisite that he, not Alison, puts out his bottom, and suffers from the red-hot iron. It is his scream for 'Water' to cool his wound that wakes the carpenter, who thinks the Flood has come and cuts his rope. The two stories are beautifully woven together. This sub-plot is a rather complex variation on the theme of the couple. It depends on two previous couples: first, the legitimate but ill-assorted and legally indissoluble union between Alison and her husband; then the illicit coupling between Alison and Nicholas. If Alison's husband had played Nicholas's part it would not have been so funny. The rivalry between two illicit lovers,

---

3   All quotations will be taken from *The Riverside Chaucer*, General Editor L.D. Benson (Oxford, 1988). The best recent discussion of the fabliaux is Charles Muscatine, *The Old French Fabliaux:* (New Haven and London, 1986). For analogues see *The Literary Context of Chaucer's Fabliaux: Texts and Translations*, ed. L.D. Benson and T.M. Andersson (Indianapolis and New York, 1971).

and their varying fortunes, make the comedy. And of course the denouement is intimately linked with the fact that it is not her husband who is in bed with Alison.

In *The Reeve's Tale* two Cambridge students take their college's wheat to be ground by the miller in Trumpington. He cheats them. They are forced, because he has released their horse, and they are too late to return to college, to spend a night with him. He, his wife and daughter, and the students all sleep in the same room. By a series of tricks the students seduce the women, but are eventually discovered and there is a hilarious fight in the bedroom. Then the students depart. Like *The Miller's Tale* it is a story wide-spread in Europe, with Italian, German, French and Flemish versions. Chaucer gives it wonderful immediacy and local realism but the structure is essentially the same in all versions. Chaucer however is unique in characterising the miller in the tale as a bully and a small-town snob, as well as dishonest, in such a way as almost to justify the students' actions. This is a story of revenge and reversal. The concept of marriage is vital, but only that the marriage may be broken as a revenge for cheating. The Miller is the biter who is bit, and the discovery is itself part of the revenge.

In *The Merchant's Tale* we have another traditional tale, though of partly learned origin. A lecherous old knight, January, wishing to make his lechery respectable, marries a young girl, May. In the course of time he becomes blind and exceedingly jealous. His squire falls in love with May and they make an assignation in a pear-tree, which is comic enough. As they begin to copulate January's sight is restored by magic. He bellows out to ask what are they doing? May has a ready answer – they are pretending, because she knew that such a pretence would restore his sight. Here the underlying point is, that a woman always has an ingenious answer, however compromising the circumstances. There is a kind of reversal her, but no revenge. The basis is the same as *The Miller's Tale* however: the instability of an old jealous husband's relation to a young wife. January is of course the biter who is bit.

In *The Shipman's Tale* a merchant lends his friend, a monk, a large sum of money. In the merchant's absence the monk seduces his wife, and gives her a sum of money to the amount of his debt. She needs the money because the merchant keeps her short. When the merchant returns and asks the monk for his money back the monk says he has already paid it to the wife. When the merchant reproaches her for not telling him, and asks his wife where it is, she says truly enough that she thought the money was for her, and she has spent it. She then consoles her husband sexually. In a sense he has asked for deceit, if we are worried by justice, but of course we are not. The neatness of the trick is amusing, and there are no consequences. The story structure here depends less on deeper contradictions in the human order, such as generational conflict, and is less enriched by Chaucer in other ways, so that it seems less imaginative than the other tales, more circumscribed and less absurd, but it too has its general point. The ancient concept of the marriage debt, which is sexual, is aligned with purely financial debt with comic effect, appropriately for a merchant. It is a traditional tale of the type called 'The Lover's Gift Regained'. Several versions including Boccaccio's (*Decameron*, VIII,1) make the deceived husband a merchant, though they also make the wife a more lecherous woman. But there is no sense of the biter bit, nor a discovery, so that this tale, brilliantly told as it is, has a less complex, and therefore less interesting, inner structure.

Chaucer tells these stories from a point of view of social superiority. He is a courtier. The audience is gentry. The agents in the story are of middling class, not gentry, except for the knight January, whose age and behaviour modifies our respect for his status. Consequently there is no social superiority felt within the tales, though in *The Merchant's Tale* May is 'of small degree' Class is only an issue if we go outside the stories to consider author and audience.[4] There is some superior intellectual amusement at ignorant men, partly by representing ignorant men sneering at clerks who then humiliate them, but this has no relationship to the couple. The lovers are types of lusty young men – students, a monk, a squire, but they are on familiar terms with their victims, and only marginally, if at all, above them in degree. January's squire is of the same class as January, the monk on terms of equality with the merchant. Students even of the King's Hall, Cambridge, such as those in *The Reeve's Tale*, were not necessarily upper-class and the Northern accents of the Cambridge students, though not an index of class, suggests a certain rustic provinciality.

It is clear enough that the basic premise of the stories is the married couple. Other couples are transient variational couplings set off against the primary couple.

In order to appreciate the complexities of the marital couple we may take a glance at views of marriage and sex expressed elsewhere in *The Canterbury Tales*, varying from the 'official' ecclesiastical culture to the 'unofficial', and secular culture.[5]

The chief spokesman for the official ecclesiastical culture is of course the

---

4 On Chaucer and class see Derek Brewer, 'Class-Distinction in Chaucer', *Tradition and Innovation in Chaucer* (London, 1982), 54-72.
5 For the use here of the notions of 'official' and 'unofficial' cultures, or sub-cultures within the general culture, see Derek Brewer, 'Gothic Chaucer', *Tradition and Innovation in Chaucer* (London, 1982), 110-36.

Parson. His so-called Tale is a meditation on Penance and the Seven Deadly Sins. The immediate source is unknown, but Siegfried Wenzel, the authoritative editor in *The Riverside Chaucer*, illustrates its traditional character. Yet it may well be that Chaucer himself put the various elements together, drawing directly or more likely indirectly on two main Latin sources written in the early thirteenth century. Of the Seven Deadly Sins Lechery is treated last, in much greater length than Gluttony but comparably with other sins. In the section following the remedy against Lechery 'sin' is taken almost wholly in a sexual sense. The actual concepts are common enough, as Brundage shows quite clearly. The Parson is a dramatic character, within the work as a whole, but his 'meditation', fully in dramatic character, is so characteristic of the mainstream of the Church's teaching that there is no sense of irony in his tale, nor of any distance between what he says and the opinions of his creator. That is not to say that these were the poet's *only* opinions, or the only opinions he was willing to present and perhaps subscribe to.

The Parson's discussion of marriage comes in the passage on Lechery and the Remedy against Lechery (*C.T.*, X, 833-935) of which I summarise some salient characteristics. Lechery is seen primarily as adultery. Simple fornication between unmarried people is barely mentioned. Marriage was made by God in heaven, but it is by adultery that the Devil wins the greater part of the world, though grim punishments follow. Lechery may also occur within marriage (a man may kill himself with his own knife). A man should love his wife like a sister. Fornication is indeed a sin, as is taking a maidenhead, for virginity is the highest estate. But the filth of adultery occupies the greater part of the section, though prostitution is also condemned. Adultery may also take place between a man and his wife when they have intercourse only for fleshly delight. Other sexual sins are then condemned.

The general remedy against Lechery is of course chastity, but the Parson refers only to chastity in marriage and widowhood. He emphasises again the lawfulness and holiness of marriage. The effect of marriage is to cleanse fornication by changing it from being a deadly sin to a venial one, performed only in the duty of replenishing the church with good stock. Marriage unites the hearts, as well as the bodies, of man and wife.

The husband is superior to the wife, but must treat her with patience and reverence. Masterful women are troublesome, as everyday experience shows, says the Parson, but wives must not on the other hand be downtrodden. They must love and obey their husbands. They must not dress too finely. They must be moderate in everything, nor laugh too much. He then turns again to the sexual aims of marriage, which are first procreation, second the yielding to each other of the marriage debt (for neither owns his or her own body, as St Paul says), and third to avoid lechery and villainy. No sexual intercourse even in marriage is without venial sin, 'because of the corruption and delight' there is in it. To have sexual intercourse, even in marriage, simply for 'amorous love' is a deadly sin, though unfortunately some people don't care how often they do it, and exert themselves to do it even beyond what appetite requires.

These orthodox views contain a powerful inner contradiction in relation to sex. Sex in marriage is good in itself (paying the debt) but also bad, a sin, even if only a venial sin when indulged in with the hope of procreation. You're not supposed to enjoy it, even though you can hardly avoid doing so. Sex is dirty. The notions of sexual desire as a kind of insanity, and sexuality as pollution, are very potent and longlasting.

Some of these points come out incidentally elsewhere in *The Canterbury Tales*. A comic use of the concept of the sinfulness of sexual desire between man and wife is made by Nicholas in *The Miller's Tale*. He places the old carpenter far away from his wife when they are up among the rafters waiting for the second Flood for, he says,

> Thy wife and thou mooste hange fer atwynne,
> For that bitwixe yow shal be no synne,
> Namoore in lookyng than ther shal in deede
>
> *C.T.*, I, 3589-91

though the true object of this is to enable Alison and Nicholas to slip away to commit adultery together.

Elsewhere it is assumed that good women do not enjoy sexual intercourse (e.g. *The Man of Law's Tale, C.T.*, II, 108-14, and *The Merchant's Tale, C.T.*, IV, 1756). Emily in *The Knight's Tale* wishes to remain a virgin, and puts it poignantly, that she does not wish to be a wife and go with child (*C.T.*, I, 2310). It is an unusually sympathetic view of women, expressed even more powerfully in the bitter, if resigned, words given to Custance in *The Man of Law's Tale*

> Women are bom to thraldom and penance
> And to been under mannes governance.
>
> *C.T.*, II, 286-7.

This gives another dimension to the concept of the couple, or rather, gives a woman's views of the Parson's, and the Church's, complacent commonplaces about the superiority of the husband in marriage. Childbirth even apart from its pain was very dangerous.

However a more positive rejection of the Church's teaching is made by Chaunticleer the cock in *The Nun's Priest's Tale* who in the service of Venus, goddess of pleasure, did all his power

> Moore for delit than world to multiplye.
>
> *C.T.*, VII, 2345.

This is part of the exquisitely absurd comedy of the tale. Nevertheless it expresses an attitude to marital sex which the Parson, and centuries of clerics, deplored as far too common. It is expressed most extensively by the Wife of Bath in her remarkable Prologue. She can 'wel understand' that 'gentil text' by which God bad us wax and multiply (*C.T.*, III, 28-9) but we are not told that she has any children and all her drift is of the pleasure of sex. That this is based on anti-feminist texts reproaching women's presumed lustfulness makes the paradox the more delightful, for it is hardly possible not to sympathise in a literary way with the Wife of Bath's lustiness, however it might be judged in real life. She cheerfully agrees that virginity is a state superior to marriage, but gladly opts for the latter. There is no more explicitly enthusiastic an advocate for marriage in the whole of English literature. She is a student of marriage, she says, and having had five hushands will welcome the sixth whenever he comes. She is also a specialist in the woe of marriage, which she has inflicted rather than suffered. Yet to her current husband, half her age, after one major bout of fisticuffs she says she is loving and true. She represents herself as having achieved harmony in marriage. Her own Tale finishes with husband and wife equally harmonious, though she adds a rider wishing always for

> Housbondes meeke, younge and fressh abedde
> And grace t'overbyde hem that we wedde.
>
> *C.T.*, IV, 1259-60

This is an interesting mirror image of what may well be supposed to be the unregenerate functional wish of many men, a succession of beautiful, docile young wives, nowadays indeed often achieved. The Wife of Bath's Prologue might be described as the first feminist manifesto in English literature. Perhaps inevitably, in terms of historical development, it is a transference to the feminine of common masculine attitudes to sex and marriage. This is not surprising since it is based on an ingenious perversion of traditional clerical mysogyny. The couple is seen as an indissoluble bond with either one partner or the other dominating. Neither love, kindness nor community of interest are necessary, though they are called for and sometimes achievable.

A more generous, but still natural attitude is expressed by the drunken Miller in the Prologue to his tale – *in vino veritas*. He promises to tell a story of how a clerk tricked a carpenter – that is, cuckolded him. The Reeve, a carpenter, complains. The Miller says there are a thousand good wives for one bad, which is the reverse of what the Wife of Bath says is proclaimed by clerics, who never praise wives. (*C.T.*, IV, 689). But the Miller goes on to say he is himself married and would not dream of taking on himself the belief that he is a cuckold. He will not consider himself one, and would no more delve inte his wife's private affairs than he would into God's. His advice as husband is that

So he may finde Goddes foyson there.
Of the remenaunt nedeth nat enquere.

C.T., I, 3145-6

The Wife of Bath used to say exactly the same thing to her old husbands, rather more bluntly (*C.T.*, III, 329-36).

For such sexually liberated people men and women seem to be equal in marriage. This attitude is only possible to those without 'honour', for there is a strong sexual element in honour, a very primitive concept but still powerful in Chaucer's imagination. While honour puts no sexual restraints on honourable men, chastity, or faithfulness in marriage, is of the essence of honour in women. A man's honour depends on his own bravery and his wife's faithfulness. Custom agreed that a man might justifiably kill his wife's lover and his unfaithful wife too. Men and women's honour are not symmetrical.[6] Adultery is not comic in such circumstances. That is one reason why Chaucer does not tell comic tales about the gentry and nobility. Honour is the source of Criseyde's shame. But non-gentry and clerics do not have honour in this strict medieval sense. (January is a knight, and his honour is just saved, but he is also a *senex amans*, always a ridiculous object.)

It is notable that though the characters apart from January in Chaucer's *fabliaux* have no honour they do not share the Miller's and Wife of Bath's relaxed atti-

---

6   Derek Brewer, 'Honour in Chaucer', *Tradition and Innovation in Chaucer* (London, 1982), 89-109.

tude towards sexual possessiveness. The husbands are violently possessive. If they were not there would be no comic tales about the couple. If there is no would-be exclusive sexual bond between the couple it might well seem that there is no couple.

This is however too limited a view of the couple in the light of Chaucer's other writings, where a bond other than sexual is envisaged. *The Franklin's Tale*, too complex to be other than briefly mentioned here, deals with honourable people, and is thus outside the limits of this paper on the *fabliaux*. *The Franklin's Tale* however deserves our passing recognition because part of its interest lies in its attempt to solve the problem of domination versus love between the married couple. When Arveragus marries Dorigen he swears that he will never take any 'maistrye' but will always obey her in all *as any lover would*

> Save that the name of soveraynetee
> That wolde he have, for shame of his degree.
>
> *C.T.*, V, 751-2

'Shame of degree' is a negative way of expressing 'honour of rank'. This is largely a social and external but none the less important factor. The husband in the eyes of the world will have mastery. In the private world of their love, she will have mastery. Love still means mastery, despite the disclaimer a few lines later (V, 765-6). All this is preceded by the wry remark that Dorigen had agreed to marry Arveragus, to take him for her husband and her lord

> Of swich lordshipe as men han over hir wyves
>
> *C.T.*, V, 743

Nature will keep on breaking in, but the framework, that provides the opportunity for the typical male jest, is the official ecclesiastical culture. The poem proceeds to set a dilemma in which promise-keeping and truth are valued above sexual faithfulness on the wife's part, but also invoke such generosity of response that the wife's chastity, and the married couple's honour, are preserved. It is the husband, though, who has to make the crucial decision.

More profound still is the concept evoked in *Troilus and Criseyde*. When Troilus has been accepted as Criseyde's lover he sings a song praising the cosmic love which holds creation together

> And couples doth in vertu for to dwelle
>
> III, 1749.

This concept is translated from the sixth-century *De Consolatione Philosophiae* of Boethius, Book II, Metre 8, of which the original version refers to the love that binds *coniugii sacrum/castis amorum*. Chaucer had slightly to adapt this, since Troilus was not married to Criseyde. But Troilus is always represented in the poem as totally committed to Criseyde; as if he were married to her. Despite some ambiguities the poem clearly illustrates the significance of the concept of the couple united by *mutual* love, which is part of the law that holds the universe together.

But what happens when love fails? The distress of this is also illustrated in *Troilus and Criseyde* when Criseyde abandons Troilus. The theme of abandonment of one lover by the other (usually men abandoning women) occurs a number of times in Chaucer's work.[7] From the point of view of the present discussion we may say that love may bring the couple together but is not always sufficient to maintain it. The law of the universe like that of man can be broken. The couple that depends on love, or at least on that kind of love best called romantic love, is likely to be transient.

The couple in Chaucer's *fabliaux* that is stable is the married couple, and that is because in the Middle Ages marriage with rare exceptions could not be dissolved. What constitutes marriage? Not love, for marriage often existed without love. Sexual intercourse was essential and marriage could be annulled if no sexual intercourse had taken place. But adultery was not grounds for divorce. There is a Canterbury Tale which even questions sexuality. *The Second Nun's Tale* of Saint Cecilia shows the saint persuading her husband that they should live together in sexual abstinence. Little is made of this but it shows that marriage could be sustained in the light of a religious love, higher than romantic love, and directed to the love of God.

But here arises the contradiction already remarked on within the view of the official culture and expressed by the Parson. Marriage is indissoluble, made by God in heaven. The spouses owe each other a sexual debt and own each other's bodies. Yet sexual love is also sinful. The couple is locked into an eternally self-contradictory set of injunctions.

Ordinary people accepted with varying degrees of comfort and evasion these contradictions, while accepting the fact of the bond that linked the couple. And this bond has to be regarded as supra-personal. It is the basic assumption of the *fabliaux*. The stories are generated mainly by the imbalances within the couple (old husband, young wife, most typically) which is then exploited by an outsider, partly hostile, partly desirous.

---

7   Derek Brewer, 'Love and Marriage in Chaucer's Poetry', *Tradition and Innovation in Chaucer* (London, 1982), 22-6.

Formally we may say in Proppian terms that the basis of the story is a situation of imbalance to which comes a protagonist (on one occasion a dual protagonist) who has a lack related to that imbalance. The lack is usually that common to young men, the lack of a woman. Unlike fairy tales the lack is remedied, not by a magic helper or donor, but by the protagonist's own ingenuity, aided and abetted by that of the young woman. The story normally ends with the lack remedied, though *The Merchant's Tale* has a slightly different pattern. The climax of the tale is not the adultery but its recognition. All is made plain and the comedy resides in that. But recognition does not alter the initial situation. The characters are basically stereotypes, but as I shall remark in a moment have some personality. The ingenuity of the plots is sympathetic to women without making them active workers in the plot, except by inference in the case of the Wife of Bath.

On the plane of content it is worth remarking that these international often bawdy popular comic tales constitute the only literature about secular married life (albeit seen as a test of, or reaction against, marriage) in European literature until the eighteenth century (e.g. Fielding's *Amelia*, 1752) unless Shakespeare's late romances be an exception. It is true that they do not give much sense of domestic harmony and comfort, though they indirectly uphold that ideal and occasionally end with it. Their sexiness ensures an audience of young as well as old, but they are not about romantic love, and their comedy creates a general perspective which is that of wryly experienced middle-age. Sexual romantic love is essentially an adolescent phase, even if one to which we may gladly regress in imagination or life. A love story if with a happy ending ends with that consummation devoutly to be wished, but as the old pun almost remarks, to consummate is to die. In every sense marriage is the end of romantic love and, we might add, the beginning of the couple.[8]

In medieval literature, and in Chaucer, there is little mention of children.[9] They are not significant as such in the *fabliaux* though the central activity surely brings them into question.

---

[8] Georges Duby, 'L'amour en France au XIIe siècle', *Mâle Moyen Age* (Paris, 1988), 43-4, remarks that 'love' was the province of the *iuvenes*. Once a man was married he joined the *seniores*, whatever his age. This by no means inhibited his sexual promiscuity according to the general understanding. A young noble who wished to remain faithful to his wife alone, even though she insisted on sexual abstinence, was regarded as ridiculous on both counts. The father's bastards were accepted readily as part of the family. The wife's were unthinkable. The mothers of the bastards were lower-class women in general, it would appear.

[9] Chaucer does include a number of references to children. Derek Brewer, 'Children in Chaucer', *Tradition and Innovation in Chaucer* (London, 1982), 46-53.

The Reeve's Tale endows the basic couple with a pair of children, somewhat improbably spread out in age, perhaps, – a twenty-year-old daughter and a baby of six months. Both children are essential in different ways to the working out of the plot, the placing of the baby's cradle being mechanically necessary, and the seduction of the daughter being one of the means (the other being the wife) of punishing the miller who is the central character.[10] They are not seen for their own sakes and as such do not affect the concept of the couple.

The absence of children reminds us of the general limitation of the concept of the couple, combined perhaps with the brevity of the *fabliaux*-form. The action in these stories is selfcontained and no consequences are envisaged. To put it at its bluntest, no one gets pregnant. They are fantasies. To this extent they have the characteristic of medieval secular romance. Romance expresses desire and wish-fulfilment – that is its strength and its weakness. In romance also no one gets pregnant. Children may be part of a family group in religious romance but they are not the consequence of the main action. Troilus and Criseyde are lovers for three years but the emotional and physical situation remains static. In real life Criseyde would surely have become pregnant. Secular romances finish with only a flourish at best towards the consequences of the couple, as for example *Havelok*, where we are assured in the final lines that they lived happily after and had fifteen children.

In the *fabliaux* we learn nothing of future possible relationships between the characters. Within the action there is no development of character, emotion or situation. Even the primary imbalance, for example, old husband/young wife, remains (necessarily) unchanged. The nature of the stories is to deal with isolated instances of the breaking of rules that most people can imagine wishing to break. As such they are as generalised and stereotyped as fantasies commonly are. Even Chaucer, whose is outstanding amongst medieval English authors in his interest in individual characterization and in connecting character with event, restricts himself to the action of the story, though he makes it much more connected and realistic than do any of the analogues. He enhances the internal realism and even naturalism of the tales as novels would do in a later period, but keeps the tales so short that they remain without consequence.

The brevity of the *fabliaux* prevents the need for moral thought and enhances the freedom of comedy. A short narrative form is in this respect only a fighting patrol into enemy territory and will necessarily retreat. It is not a set-piece attack to conquer new moral ground in the name of immorality. It is possible for a short form to relate pathetic or horrible events, as do *The Physician's, Pardoner's* and

---

10 Derek Brewer, 'The Reeve's Tale', *Chaucer's Frame Tales*, ed. J.O. Fichte (Cambridge, 1987).

Manciple's Tales (also of folkloric type, incidentally) but these too are self-contained, anecdotal fantasies, with no significant consequences. In so far as a moral is to be drawn, they are of the nature of *exempla*.

The brevity of a short form limits the possibilities of the reader's full sympathetic identification with any of the characters. This is of especial advantage with comedy, which requires a peculiar mixture of detachment from and identification with the characters. We need to share in imagination their experience and emotion, yet also to be able to stand back with sufficient detachment to laugh at frustration, failure, injustice, etc. This ambivalence of approach is part of the experience, both subjective and objective, of incongruity within juxtaposition which creates the essential ambivalence of comedy. In a short form dealing with basic stereotypes (however differentiated by Chaucer's genius) we easily recognise and identify with the characters sufficiently to have some fellow-feeling; but there is not space or time in the poem to identify with them very fully. We are more or less on the side of the young, unscrupulous, clever and beautiful, but we are as easily amused when these fine young animals are themselves tricked as when we see them tricking those who are old, ugly, quarrelsome, jealous, or otherwise riding for a fall.

The ambivalent attitude to characters and events may be summed up in the middle-aged resignation (and envy) of such remarks as 'boys will be boys', especially while girls are girls. There is no attack on morality, though these tales are concerned with very familiar kinds of immorality. Nor is there a new morality propounded which is the old immorality writ large. The standard medieval morality is accepted, but with a toleration for the imagination of natural infringements of a kind amply documented in ecclesiastical records, as really occurring, and such as were the despair of the clergy (when they were not committing such sins themselves).

The ambivalence and, for the literal-minded, the inconsistencies, of such an attitude with regard to general values and experience of the world corresponds with a certain complexity in the literary nature of these stories, especially of Chaucer's *fabliaux*. The stories are a mixture of romance and materialism, that is, a mixture of wish-fulfilment, with recognition of that basically physical aspect of life which later became the special domain of the novel. Though these international popular comic tales are fantasies they have a clear place in the development of the early modern novel. But the novel takes us beyond the brevity of the medieval short narrative form requiring much more individualistic characterization and a richer cast than that of the couple, even if the creation of the couple is often the ultimate aim of the plot.

The couple, indissolubly linked, itself potentially in human terms that inescapable juxtaposition of incongruous elements which is of the essence of comedy, constitutes the essential basis of these particular *fabliaux*. The couple is linked in a union which may include but extends beyond sex and love. The concept of the couple is the social and formal base of those stories which fantasise our obsession with, our desire to escape from, and our need always to re-create, both personally and socially, that elusive entity, the couple.

Members and Associate Members of the Symposium

Flemming G. Andersen
Ida Anine Andersen
Sverre Bagge
Birgitte Balsløv
Karen Margrethe Banke
Connie Beck
Hans Bekker-Nielsen
Walter Blank
Marianne Børch
Derek Brewer
Birte Carlé
Fridtjof Jacob Pauli Christiansen
Ulla Christoffersen
Jan Dietrichson
Mats Edvardsson
Dorrit Einersen
Rita Geertz
J. Gerritsen
Andreas Haarder
Joseph Harris
Paul Horstmann
Jacob Isager
Eric Jacobsen
Jørgen Højgaard Jørgensen

Margit Kaad Johansen
Karin Lidell
Julia McGrew
Kajsa Meyer
Raul Mordenti
Morten Nøjgaard
Tore Nyberg
Esther Nyholm
Jens E. Olesen
Michel Olsen
Ivar Orgland
Rita Pedersen
Thomas Pettitt
Iørn Piø
Margit Lave Rønsholdt
Kurt Schier
Reinhold Schröder
Barbro Söderberg
Leif Søndergaard
Olav Solberg
Anette Thingholm
Henrik Tvarnø
Kirsten Vittrup